D1255189

THE TWO VOICES

THE TWO VOICES

A Tennyson Study

by

ELTON EDWARD SMITH

UNIVERSITY OF NEBRASKA PRESS · LINCOLN

Publishers on the Plains

Copyright © 1964 by the University of Nebraska Press

ALL RIGHTS RESERVED

Library of Congress Catalog card number 64–11349

PR5581
.S5

Manufactured in the United States of America

To

A. McKinley Terhune

Scholar, teacher, friend

Contents

45953

Acknowledgments

I am indebted to friends, teachers, and colleagues who have read this study in manuscript and left a residue of invaluable comment, criticism, and suggestion. Dr. A. McKinley Terhune read so closely and so frequently that it is entirely possible that he knows portions of the study more exactly than the author. Professor Dorothy Drew, Professor Leonard Brown, Dr. James H. Elson, Dr. Sanford B. Meech, Dr. Arthur W. Hoffman, Dr. Malcolm MacLaren, and Dr. Donald A. Dike read, made notations, and added the warmth of discussion to the points in question. More recently, Dr. Robert L. Zetler raised the important issue of author's point of view, and Dr. Sheldon N. Grebstein contributed stylistic suggestions as well as a handsome, six-volume edition of Tennyson's poetical works. Dr. William D. Templeman and Dr. Louis Crompton also read this study in manuscript; their analyses were most helpful—and in some cases provocative.

Of course the research involved would have been quite impossible without the ample Victorian resources of the Syracuse University Library and the gracious cooperation of librarians there and at the University of South Florida.

I am particularly grateful to the members of the old village Baptist Church of Camillus, New York, who were generous in support and kind in understanding while their pastor pounded out this manuscript in the study of their parsonage.

ELTON EDWARD SMITH

The Two Voices

Introduction

In *Essays, Ancient and Modern*, Thomas Stearns Eliot called Alfred Tennyson "a great poet for reasons that are perfectly clear. He has three qualities which are seldom found together except in the greatest poets: abundance, variety, and complete competence."[1]

The "abundance" of a poet who wrote from early childhood until his death at the age of eighty-three is clear to all. His "variety" is attested to by Stephen Gwynn in a *Spectator* article for March 22, 1946: "If I had to defend myself for praising Tennyson, I should dwell on the range and variety of his output. Few poets in the world have done so many things so well as Tennyson. . . ."[2] Mr. Eliot magnificently supports his own claim of Tennyson's competence with a bit of florid criticism: "whatever he sets out to do, he succeeds in doing. . . . He had the finest ear of any English poet since Milton. . . . *Maud* and *In Memoriam* are each a series of poems, given form by the greatest lyrical resourcefulness that a poet has ever shown. . . . Tennyson is the great master of metric as well as of melancholia . . . the saddest of all English poets, among the Great in Limbo, the most instinctive rebel against the society in which he was the most perfect conformist."[3]

But despite the bravura of praise, the tone is noticeably defensive. Mr. Gwynn felt he might have to "defend" himself

---

[1] Thomas Stearns Eliot, *Essays, Ancient and Modern* (New York, 1936), p. 175.

[2] Stephen Gwynn, "The Return to Tennyson," *Spectator*, CLXXVI (March 22, 1946), 293.

[3] Eliot, *Essays*, pp. 175 ff.

I

for praising Tennyson. Reasons that are flatly called "perfectly clear" often require a great deal of proof to make them seem even comparatively clear. The abundance and metrical competence of Tennyson's poetry do not provide the area of attack; it is the variety of type and topic which has given rise to conflicting critical estimates. The following pages review nine significant critical attempts which have been made in the past forty years to explain and interpret Tennyson to the twentieth-century reader.

The first such attempt was made with the kindest of intentions—to revive enthusiasm for Tennyson's poetry by discarding large parts of it. In 1922, Sir Harold Nicolson's *Tennyson: Aspects of His Life, Character and Poetry* [4] divided Tennyson's poetic career into four main periods. The first "imitative Keatsian" era of luxuriant versification ran from 1827 to 1842, beginning with *Poems by Two Brothers* in 1827 and ending with the two-volume *Poems* of 1842. The second, somewhat overlapping, period was the most "important lyrical" period, 1835–1855, including "The Two Voices" and "Break, Break, Break" from the 1842 volumes; *The Princess* in 1847; *In Memoriam, A. H. H.*, 1850; and "Ode on the Death of the Duke of Wellington," 1852. The third he designated the most "unfortunate, mid-Victorian period," 1857–1879, judging *Enoch Arden* in 1864, the first seven *Idylls of the King*, and the first three plays all guilty by association. In the fourth, "the splendid Aldworth period," 1880–1892, the sunset glow of a poet in his seventies and eighties illuminated *Ballads and Other Poems*, 1880, "Rizpah," "Lucknow," "De Profundis," "Tiresias," "The Ancient Sage," and "To E. FitzGerald."

It is immediately apparent that this is not a strictly chronological grouping. The "important lyrical period" goes back seven years into the "imitative Keatsian era." The second and third periods miss *Maud* entirely. The "splendid" fourth

[4] Sir Harold Nicolson, *Tennyson: Aspects of His Life, Character and Poetry* (Boston, 1922), pp. 229 ff.

period actually includes the later five *Idylls of the King*—the first seven of which were enrolled in the fraternity of the damned as "unfortunate" and "mid-Victorian"—as well as three plays (the same number as in the preceding "unfortunate" period), and *Locksley Hall Sixty Years After*.

It also becomes clear that this is a value judgment based upon Sir Harold Nicolson's requirements for modern poetry ("I think it may be said without fear of contradiction that what the early twentieth century primarily demands from poetry is a reality of emotional impulse"),[5] upon a dichotomy between the prosperous Isle of Wight Victorian and the black-mooded, melancholy mystic of Lincolnshire, as well as upon his own variation on the celebrated theme of "betrayal": ". . . the great lyric poet who had been born up there among the Lincolnshire wolds, had been . . . tamed, controlled, labelled, and given a function unnatural to his genius; the wild, unhappy animal that lurked within him had been caged and shackled, and the real intention and meaning of the man had been forever veiled—even from himself." [6]

Essentially Nicolson's critical position isolated two chronological periods (1835–1855 and 1880–1892) as acceptable to modern poetic taste, and one mood—melancholy—as the true and natural complexion of the poet's mind. This position is very important for two reasons: first because it is so partial, and second because it has provided the pattern for much of the later criticism. A very lively corpse that will not stay buried, it revives in strange and embarrassing places. It is, of course, a twentieth-century relative of Matthew Arnold's nineteenth-century dictum on Thomas Gray—"had his lot fallen among other circumstances, or in a less cloying age. . . ."

In 1923, the year after Nicolson's book was published, Hugh I'Anson Fausset, also a spokesman of modernity, quoted Tennyson's characteristically dubious remark after he had heard the boy choristers of Westminster Abbey—"It is

5 *Ibid.*, p. 27.
6 *Ibid.*, p. 25.

beautiful, but what empty, awful mockery if there were no God." Then the critic proceeded to explain:

Such uneasy thoughts rise in a mind, when beauty is experienced, not as an expression of truth and of God, but as a sensational stimulus or a sentimental narcotic.

Tennyson was an imperfect poet to the extent that he failed to realize the identity of truth and beauty. It was because both the beauty and the morality of the Victorian age were, through selfishness, imperfectly related to truth, that men slid imperceptibly into the abyss. And while, on the fields of Flanders, there was no God, the mockery and squalor of it all was relieved by no white-robed choristers, voicing a consolatory strain.[7]

When Sir Edmund Gosse objected, Fausset replied in the preface to the Travellers' Library Edition of 1929: "Tennyson allowed himself to float upon the impure stream of contemporary public opinion, and so to reflect, at one time even to encourage, that combination of arrogance and panic, which the thoughtless have called 'Patriotism' and the honest 'Jingoism.' That spirit and the repercussions it begot, in my opinion, contributed to the catastrophe of 1914. All I have remarked is that Tennyson, with all his moral affirmations, never till his old age, when it was too late, and even then dubiously, raised his very public voice in protest." [8]

From the date and tone of the criticism it is clear that Mr. Fausset was a member of that generation which was eager to place the blame for war, with the hope that by exposing the villains war would be no more. But in this criticism, he, as a child of the early twentieth century, accuses the poet of being a child of the nineteenth century. Percy Bysshe Shelley had noted, less passionately and more thoughtfully, in his Preface to *The Revolt of Islam,* "a resemblance which does not depend upon their own will between all the writers of any particular

[7] Hugh I'Anson Fausset, *Tennyson: A Modern Portrait* (London, 1923), p. 302.

[8] *Ibid.,* p. iii.

age. They cannot escape from subjection to a common influence which arises out of an infinite combination of circumstances belonging to the times in which they live; though each is in a degree the author of the very influence by which his being is thus pervaded." And as Mr. Eliot wrote, although he might be shocked to be found in agreement with a Romantic poet, "It happens now and then that a poet, by some strange accident, expresses the mood of his generation, at the same time that he is expressing a mood of his own which is quite remote from that of his generation. This is not a question of insincerity: there is an amalgam of yielding and opposition below the level of consciousness." [9]

T. S. Eliot's influential essay of 1936 on *In Memoriam*, from which the salient points have already been quoted, places him on the side of both appreciation and partition. Notwithstanding all the superlative rhetoric of "finest ear," "greatest lyrical resourcefulness," and "great master of metric," he goes on to add: "as well as of melancholia . . . saddest of all English poets . . . rebel . . . conformist." The black, unhappy mystic has been revived, but with significant additions. We presume that on the point of melancholia, Mr. Eliot would agree with an article written by Nicolson in 1942: "The poems that we admire today come straight from the undiverted springs of his true genius. We do not admire his message of tenderness or comfort or complacency; we admire his moments of anguish, gloom and doubt." [10] But Eliot's additions are important: Tennyson is also a great poet, a metrical master, and his work reveals a tension between societal rebellion and conformity.

W. H. Auden, in the introduction to a selection of Tennyson's poems published in 1944, gave further circulation to Nicolson's caveat—"central lyrical throb," "deep, original

---

[9] Eliot, *Essays*, p. 184. *The Complete Poetical Works of Percy Bysshe Shelley* (ed.), Thomas Hutchinson (London, 1948), p. 35.

[10] Sir Harold Nicolson, "Marginal Comment," *Spectator*, CLXIX (October 9, 1942), 334.

poetic temperament . . . shallow, timid practical intelligence," [11] and passed on Eliot's coin as well: "he had the finest ear, perhaps, of any English poet; he was also undoubtedly the stupidest; there was little about melancholia that he didn't know; there was little else that he did." [12]

Paull F. Baum's *Tennyson Sixty Years After* [13] is described by Jerome Hamilton Buckley as "scholarly but hostile" [14] and by John Killham as "a book giving the impression of having been written out of a sense of having a painful duty to perform." [15] Baum borrowed the term "melancholy" [16] from Eliot and the charge of "mediocre intellectual endowment" [17] from Nicolson and Auden, but his chief criticisms were directed at Tennyson's attempts to fuse the aesthetic and the moral, and he expressed an Arnoldian attitude toward a poet who tried to deal with the problems of his own time. As Killham remarks, "the whole book takes as its basic assumption that Tennyson pretended to be *sacer Victorianus vates*, and this Mr. Baum cannot forget, and clearly cannot forgive." [18] The tendency toward partition that we have already noted in Nicolson, Eliot, and Auden is also present in this book when Professor Baum writes so confidently: "and now, since we are far enough removed to recognize the difference, we are able to separate the 'true' from the 'false' [poetry] and to see how, his instinct being for beauty, the necessity of finding in contemporary life subjects to write about led him to beautify inferior material." [19]

[11] Nicolson, *Tennyson: Aspects*, p. 9.

[12] Wystan Hugh Auden, Introduction, *A Selection from the Poems of Alfred, Lord Tennyson* (Garden City, 1944), p. x.

[13] Paull F. Baum, *Tennyson Sixty Years After* (Chapel Hill, 1948).

[14] Jerome Hamilton Buckley, *Tennyson: The Growth of a Poet* (Cambridge, Mass., 1960), p. viii.

[15] John Killham (ed.), *Critical Essays on the Poetry of Tennyson* (London, 1960), p. 16.

[16] Baum, *Tennyson Sixty Years After*, p. vii.   [17] *Ibid.*, p. vii.

[18] Killham (ed.), *Critical Essays*, p. 17.

[19] Baum, *Tennyson Sixty Years After*, pp. vii–viii.

Frank Laurence Lucas' comparison of Browning and Tennyson in *Ten Victorian Poets* (1948) [20] is a classic of comparative criticism, but it broke no actually new ground in the interpretation of Tennyson himself. In *Tennyson*, published in 1957, he faintly echoed the Nicolson dogma of the lyrical poet spoiled by the didactic mold: "by nature he was passionately absorbed in the riddles of the painful earth; as he grew prominent, the prophet's mantle was thrust upon him, and at times, one may feel, his song grew smothered by it." [21] But he did present two quite fresh critical suggestions in the areas of nonrationalism and dualism. "Why read him for his 'thought'? —why not like Sappho, or Catullus, or Ronsard, for his poetry?" [22] And within a few pages, in a magnificent paragraph which will be quoted in full in Chapter V, he delineated what he called the "Double Character of Tennyson." [23] The point of view expressed there becomes definitive for this study.

In *The Alien Vision of Victorian Poetry*, 1952, Edward Dudley Hume Johnson inverted the representative character of Tennyson by insisting that the quality which makes him representative is "that very quality of intransigeance as a result of which he repudiated his society and sought refuge from the spirit of the times in the better ordered realm of interior consciousness." [24] At the beginning of the nineteenth century the poet could still wage warfare on prejudice and materialism and assert the transcendental authority of the poetic vision. But with the appearance of the Pre-Raphaelites, the artist had come to recognize and regret his ineffectiveness in influencing the lives of his contemporaries, except for that small coterie of initiates who valued the form of art quite apart from its message. Johnson reasoned that in the changing climate of the Victorian Age, Tennyson, Browning, and

---

[20] Frank Laurence Lucas, *Ten Victorian Poets* (New York, 1948).

[21] Frank Laurence Lucas, *Tennyson* (London, 1957), p. 9.

[22] *Ibid.*, p. 6.   [23] *Ibid.*, p. 13.

[24] Edward Dudley Hume Johnson, *The Alien Vision of Victorian Poetry* (Princeton, 1952), p. ix.

Arnold all learned to make concessions to literary fashions of which they did not personally approve in order "to gain a wide audience and play an influential part in the life of the times"; but that along with that conformity, they developed "remarkable techniques for sublimating private insights without materially falsifying the original perceptions at the heart of the creative impulse." [25] The conformity mechanism of this formula bears an obvious relationship to Browning's condemnation of Wordsworth—"he chose the easier and more prosperous course: he became the Laureate of his age." Johnson's theory of the sublimation of private insight in public statement is interesting in relation to the question of Archbishop Trench, "when except in our times, did men seek to build up their poetry on their own individual experiences, instead of some objective foundations common to all men?" [26] It also bears upon the distinction that Robert Langbaum draws between two sorts of literature: "that which deals in objectively verifiable meanings by exhibiting actions assessable because they can be related to a stable moral system, generally consented to; and that which is appropriate to an age without beliefs generally subscribed to, 'a literature which returns upon itself, making its own values only to dissolve them before the possibility of judgment, turning them into biographical phenomena, manifestations of a life which as life is self-justifying.'" [27] Johnson's own discussion of Tennyson, Browning, and Arnold placed them among the last poets to seek a place in the popular culture, but still cultivating what he calls "a double awareness" to satisfy the broad demands of the prevailing social spirit, with which they often agree, because they wished to incorporate in their poetry insights of "different and sometimes contradictory import." [28] It will be

[25] *Ibid.*, p. xv.

[26] M. Trench, *Richard Chenevix Trench, Archbishop: Letters and Memorials* (London, 1888), I, 73.

[27] Robert Langbaum, *The Poetry of Experience* (London, 1957), p. 92.

[28] E. D. H. Johnson, *The Alien Vision*, p. xiii.

noted immediately that the "double awareness" of which he writes is part of the same vein of thought which Eliot uncovered as the rebellion-conformity tension and which Lucas called the "double character" of Tennyson.

John Killham published *Tennyson and "The Princess": Reflections of an Age* with exactly the opposite intention from that of Professor Baum. "It is quite mistaken to think that it [*The Princess*] is a melodious and overwrought poetical recommendation of a reactionary and even silly solution of what was called the 'woman-question.' In fact, it is time that the still popular belief that Tennyson was a good poet for some things, but inclined to give in to a supposed demand for poetic 'narcotics' was disposed of." [29] He also took issue with Johnson and Fausset on the question of conformity: "that he was intending to reach a wide public is shown by his careful omission of much of the scientific matter which in poems earlier in date of composition was allowed to appear, and also by his using for the narrative part of his poem a story of a very popular sort at the time. But his motive is not satisfactorily accounted for, in my view, by those cynical critics who regard a bid for a wide audience as no more than a wish for popular success and large profits. . . . he sought a wide audience because he believed his reasons deserved it." [30]

In 1960, Killham edited a collection of *Critical Essays on the Poetry of Tennyson* [31] which made available periodical articles by Arthur J. Carr, H. M. McLuhan, G. Robert Stange, Elizabeth Hillman Waterston, Lionel Stevenson, E. J. Chiasson, Graham Hough, Leo Spitzer, an introduction and one of his own articles, and essays from T. S. Eliot, G. M. Young, and Cleanth Brooks. This collection is memorable because of the number of its writers who refuse to share the main critical tendency of Tennyson-partition and who find

[29] John Killham, *Tennyson and "The Princess": Reflections of an Age* (London, 1958), p. 2.

[30] *Ibid.*, p. 4.

[31] Killham (ed.), *Critical Essays*.

values and significant interpretations throughout his total work. Some of these will be referred to in the following pages.

The last modern works to be considered in this brief review of criticism are two books by Jerome Hamilton Buckley: the first a general study, *The Victorian Temper: A Study in Literary Culture*,[32] 1951, and the second, *Tennyson: The Growth of a Poet*,[33] 1960. The clue to his treatment of Tennyson in the former work is the location of the chapter, "Tennyson—'The Two Voices,'" between Chapter III, "The Spasmodic School," and Chapter V, "The Pattern of Conversion." "In his early work we see both the Spasmodic impulse that culminated in *Maud* and the 'anti-romantic' bias that produced a sociological aesthetic."[34] Thus, as related to the previous chapter, Tennyson turned away from aestheticism and the frenzy of the Spasmodics toward an antiromantic, socially responsible maturity. In Chapter V, Buckley reads *In Memoriam* as part of the general pattern of nineteenth-century conversion.

Far from unpremeditated, its "wild and wandering cries" traced the soul's growth from unshadowed hope through the denial of life itself towards the final conquest of doubt and despair. By painful stages the poet learned to transcend an isolating self-consciousness, to achieve the saner perspective of dispassion, and ultimately to accept the tragic realities of an objective world: [This is the closest Buckley comes to a definition of the "nineteenth-century pattern of conversion."]

> I will not shut me from my kind,
>   And lest I stiffen into stone,
>   I will not eat my heart alone,
> Nor feed with sighs a passing wind.

Through a determined social dedication, he rose above the paralysis of private grief, the stone-stiff inactivity which was death itself. Life, he concluded, could have meaning only if it

[32] Jerome Hamilton Buckley, *The Victorian Temper: A Study in Literary Culture* (Cambridge, Mass., 1951).

[33] Buckley, *Tennyson*.

[34] Buckley, *The Victorian Temper*, p. 68.

were brought into harmony with the "eternal process moving one," with the purposes of all creation evolving slowly from form to form towards "one far-off divine event."[35]

Thus Tennyson became for Buckley the neat link between the Spasmodics and the poets he included in the conversion pattern.

Clearly Buckley's volume on Tennyson was haunted by the vigorous ghost of his three chapters in the general study. On page 141 he describes the hero of *Maud* and the narrator of "Locksley Hall" as kinsmen "of the 'Spasmodic' protagonist like Alexander Smith's Walter or Sydney Dobell's Balder." The phrase "conversion pattern" does not appear, but the central thesis of the book hinges on the proposition that after *In Memoriam* Tennyson had overcome his doubts.

Whatever its public overtone, *In Memoriam* was written to satisfy a private need, and as a whole it occupies a place in Tennyson's own development comparable to that of *The Prelude* in the career of Wordsworth. Like *The Prelude*, which appeared posthumously in the same year, it describes the loss of hope and the recovery of assent, the reassertion of the dedicated spirit; it grounds a new faith on the persistence of the remembered past; and it freely reorders literal facts to achieve its psychological pattern, to illustrate "the growth of a poet's mind," or, as Tennyson called it, "the way of the soul."[36]

The "recovery of assent" is a highly affirmative way to describe the progress of the elegies in *In Memoriam*. After noting the "epiphany" of the crucial Poem XCV, Dr. Buckley states more than really can be claimed: "eventually the trance is 'stricken thro' with doubt'; the appearances of the world in all its 'doubtful dusk' obscure the vision, and the poet returns to awareness of simple physical sensation. Yet he brings with him renewed purpose and composure, his experience has given him the certitude that 'science' could not establish and therefore cannot destroy . . . though unable to sustain his vision,

<hr/>

[35] *Ibid.*, pp. 88 ff.　　[36] Buckley, *Tennyson*, p. 108.

the 'I' of the poem finds in his mystical insight the surest warrant for spiritual recovery." [37]

An "epiphany" "stricken thro' with doubt"; "a trance . . . cancell'd"—these scarcely add up to the total of "certitude." They should be more simply interpreted: in occasional mystical moments the poet is caught up in real fellowship with his dead friend, but then doubt returns, his vision departs and he is back again with his everyday questions and fears. Dr. Buckley admits that Coventry Patmore reported, after a visit to Coniston in the summer of 1850, that *In Memoriam* gave a "defective notion" [38] of Tennyson's true religious conviction. Of course he must have been aware that in reading the poem to Mr. J. T. Knowles, Tennyson had asserted, "It's too hopeful, this poem, more than I am myself. . . ." [39] Yet he plainly states that Tennyson could not make progress with the *Idylls of the King* because of his lack of belief, [40] and thus implies that when he did actually compose with "assurance" [41] it was because he had conquered his doubts. Although Dr. Buckley's book is beautifully written and richly annotated, the thesis of a growth that required the conquest of doubt and the attainment of serene assent simply cannot be maintained. Most modern critics do not share Dr. Buckley's affirmative reading of the issue of doubt and faith in *In Memoriam*.

Douglas Bush's *Mythology and the Romantic Tradition*, [42] gave a rather succinct outline of the mainstream of critical comment up to 1937:

The common pattern of interpretation is something like this. Tennyson began as a genuine romantic poet and ended as a Laureate, a British minister for divine affairs, who aspired to see his Pilot face to face, "as gentleman to gentleman." The

[37] *Ibid.*, p. 123.   [38] *Ibid.*, p. 127.

[39] W. M. Rolfe (ed.), *The Complete Poetical Works of Tennyson* (Cambridge, Mass., 1898), p. 832.

[40] Buckley, *Tennyson*, p. 151.   [41] *Ibid.*, p. 170.

[42] Douglas Bush, *Mythology and the Romantic Tradition* (Cambridge, Mass., 1937), pp. 197–228.

real poetic fire that he possessed was gradually extinguished, it seems, by a number of causes—native timidity and morbid sensitiveness to both praise and blame; the Apostles' contagious zeal for uplift; hostile reviewers; the thrusting, by misguided friends and pious public, of the role of *vates* or preacher upon a born singer; the paralyzing result of accepting and expounding the Victorian compromise; the taming influence of a wife who ruled his spirit from her sofa; prosperity and familiar acquaintance with Royalty.[43]

On the next page, he goes on to refute this "common pattern": "A complete survey of Tennyson's life from Somersby to Westminster Abbey does not suggest that he was notably warped, that he took or was pushed into the wrong road. . . . There are paradoxes in the mature Tennyson, but there were paradoxes in little Alfred, who was a combination of normal boy, scholar, poet, melancholist and mystic. . . . If one allows for the normal mellowing of maturity, Tennyson was at the end what he was at the beginning . . . ."[44]

So much for "irresponsible, indolent reviewers,"[45] those "barbarous people" who were "blind to the magic" and "deaf to the melody," who "snarl'd at and cursed me."[46] This study does not propose to echo critical judgments in terms of "lyricism" rather than "didacticism"; the smothered song of a natural singer; "finest ear," "stupidest" poet; the "true" or the "false" Tennyson; nor does it, with Buckley, seek to establish a conversion pattern. Instead, taking the clues of Eliot, Lucas, and Johnson, it points to a recognition of those tensions which run through his entire work and which, by their very nature, cannot be released or stressed on either pole, but must be accepted as the continued strain of opposites.

If some modern criticism keeps insisting upon fragmentation and partition, other criticism is at least equally certain that segmentation is wrong. In 1939, Bernard Groom attested to

[43] *Ibid.*, p. 197.   [44] *Ibid.*, pp. 198–199.
[45] "(Hendecasyllabics)."   [46] "Merlin and the Gleam," III.

the continuity of Tennyson's diction. "There were no profound changes in Tennyson's diction during the course of his long poetic career. . . . Tennyson attained a characteristic style early in his career and he never lost it. . . . Naturally there was some change and development in the course of so long a life, but much less than in that of some other poets. . . . One might illustrate the essentials of Tennyson's diction from the 1842 volume alone." [47]

Also in 1939, G. M. Young commented, " 'The ground-flame of the crocus breaks the mould'—That is Tennyson at twenty. It might be Tennyson at eighty." [48] Arthur J. Carr wrote, "In the early poems the underlying theme of the 'divided will' is charged with the highest imaginative excitement, and most of the issues that were to be explored later are set forth." [49] In 1957, in the fourth volume of his monumental *Religious Trends in English Poetry: 1830–1880*, Hoxie Neale Fairchild doubted "the possibility of dismembering Tennyson into 'real' and 'laureate,' or 'early' and 'late.' Even in his querulous and disappointed old age his fundamental beliefs and aspirations were those of his youth. . . . His ideas as well as his moods are different in different poems, the inconsistencies appear in each of the 'periods' into which students have vainly tried to divide his career." [50]

In 1960, John Killham stated in his introduction to the *Critical Essays on the Poetry of Tennyson* that "the remarkably clear rise-and-fall pattern of Wordsworth's work obviously does not fit Yeats: nor does it fit Tennyson. Tennyson is a

[47] Bernard Groom, "On the Diction of Tennyson, Browning and Arnold," *Society for Pure English*, Tract No. LIII (Oxford, 1939), 97–98.

[48] George M. Young, "The Age of Tennyson," Warton Lecture, *Proceedings of the British Academy*, XXV (1939); also Killham (ed.), *Critical Essays*, p. 45.

[49] Arthur J. Carr, "Tennyson as a Modern Poet," *University of Toronto Quarterly*, XIX (July 1950), 361–382; also Killham (ed.), *Critical Essays*, p. 45.

[50] Hoxie Neale Fairchild, *Religious Trends in English Poetry: 1830–1880* (New York, 1957), IV, 102, 112.

poet whose sources of strength lay deep in his personality and came forth in a hundred streams, some piddling, some large but lazy, a few shining and pure. And they did so all his life." [51] G. Robert Stange mentioned that "the tensions—and the richness—which mark Tennyson's early work can be found at the end as well as at the beginning of the collected poems." [52] In this study, it is these tensions and the consequent enrichment of Tennyson's poetry that interest us. To illustrate the delineation of inner tensions, five poems which stretch across thirty-three years of composition may be cited: "Nothing will Die," "All Things will Die," "The Two Voices," "Milton," "The Progress of Spring."

In *Poems, Chiefly Lyrical,* 1830, the youthful poet published two companion-pieces, "Nothing will Die" and "All Things will Die." In *Demeter and Other Poems,* 1889, the eighty-year-old poet published two companion-pieces, "Forlorn" and "Happy." Amidst his juvenilia, there was that balancing and pairing-off, that tension between affirmation and denial that was to be characteristic throughout a long and celebrated career. In the former pieces, "Nothing was born; / Nothing will die; / All things will change" is perfectly balanced by "All things were born. / Ye will come never more, / For all things must die." This is the record of a youthful mind which saw both obverse and reverse of every coin, and was still seeing them both fifty-nine years later. Each position must be stated, each evokes its appropriate poetic emotion and imagery, each is persuasive in its way, and the outcome is not synthesis but stalemate.

In the winter of 1833, Tennyson wrote the poem which contributes the title to this study, "The Two Voices." It was a time "of great depression consequent upon the death of his sister." [53] "I was so utterly miserable, a burden to myself and

[51] Killham (ed.), *Critical Essays,* p. 3.

[52] G. Robert Stange, "Tennyson's Mythology—a Study of 'Demeter and Persephone,'" *English Literary History,* XXI (Baltimore, 1954), 67.

[53] Rolfe (ed.), *Complete Poetical Works,* p. 30.

to my family, that I said, 'Is life worth anything?'"[54] was Tennyson's own comment on the state of mind that produced the poem. With the original title "The Thoughts of a Suicide,"[55] it greatly resembles the Jesuit dialogues of the Counter Reformation between an advocate of heaven and an *advocatus diaboli*—but with the significant difference that in the latter the advocate of heaven always won. The two voices of Tennyson's poem are the voice of despair and the voice of hope. For one hundred and thirty-three stanzas of three lines each, the poet is engaged in debate with the voice of despair. He presents all the premises for the value of life that are inherent in the philosophical tradition of the western world. Referring to the Bible, he claims that life is of positive value because man is "wonderfully made," the crown of creation with "dominion" over all created things, and that each individual is of infinite worth. Then drawing inspiration from the nineteenth-century idea of progress, he states the positive value of living in order to see change and development in the life of man and of the world. Backed into personalism, he pleads the severe social judgment on the suicide and brings out his youthful dream of a useful, heroic life, and a death which would be regretted by men. In anger, he insists that the world does have the record of some few heroic lives. Desperately he produces the mystery of man's immemorial hope of eternity. Routed from immortality after death, he shoots the "random arrow" of his defense toward the dim dream of pre-existence. At last, abandoning argument, the poet cries that in spite of all human misery and despair, "more" and "fuller" life is what he desires.

The "still, small voice" has logic, the facts of the material universe, and the hard dicta of common sense on his side. The poet blares the trumpets of idealism and beats the tattoo of heroism; his adversary always speaks quietly, reasonably,

[54] Hallam, Lord Tennyson, *Alfred, Lord Tennyson: A Memoir by His Son* (New York, 1897), I, 193 n.

[55] *Ibid.*, I, 193 n.

monotonously. Man is no more wonderful than any other part of creation, he is infinitely small in the infinite largeness of interstellar space, he is an expendable one among the teeming many, he will age while nature remains ever young; because the scale is so vast, man's progress is never appreciably advanced; the poet need not invoke heroic tales because his is a weak, divided temperament, he is just an ineffectual dreamer, not little lower than the angels, but a wailer, a brawler, creeping inch by inch through the dark, and his father before him lived the same "life of nothings"; pain and unrest and misery are more real than shadowy mirages of pre-existence, and the only antidote for the evil of life is restful death.

The "turning point" of the poem is indicated by the ringing of church bells, the recognition of Sabbath morn, and the sight of a happy family on the way to church. These auditory and visual symbols of God, faith, human love, and human generation are the objective correlative which restores the poet to the world of meanings he has hitherto known. W. Stacy Johnson coupled this resolution with the Epithalamium at the close of *In Memoriam* as evidence of the value Tennyson placed upon marriage.[56] But it is important to note that although these images may perform a poetic resolution, they are in no sense a solution of the problem; the war is not ended— a mere armistice has been signed. In the brief (five three-line stanzas) dialogue with the voice of hope, the arguments of despair are never answered, the poet's doubts are never laid. Instead, the poet's reasons are replaced by the poet's emotions, and the reasons of the voice of hope remain "hidden."

> in that hour
> From out my sullen heart a power
> Broke, like the rainbow from the shower,
> To feel, altho' no tongue can prove,
> That every cloud, that spreads above
> And veileth love, itself is love. [lines 442–447]

[56] W. Stacy Johnson, "The Theme of Marriage in Tennyson," *Victorian Newsletter*, XII (Fall 1957), 10.

In this regard the poem of 1833, written when the poet was twenty-four, delineates in miniature the exact pattern of the great elegy of 1850, published when the poet was forty-one. Dark reason has all the best of the argument, weak faith rises on bright-hued but ineffectual wings, the final outcome of logic is the abandonment of logic, and faith is rooted far deeper in feeling than in vision. "To feel," in the passage just quoted from "The Two Voices," exactly equals "I have felt" from *In Memoriam*:

> If e'er when faith had fallen asleep,
>   I heard a voice, "believe no more,"
>   And heard an ever-breaking shore
> That tumbled in the Godless deep,
>
> A warmth within the breast would melt
>   The freezing reason's colder part,
>   And like a man in wrath the heart,
> Stood up and answer'd, "I have felt."
>
>   [CXXIV]

Tennyson was a hearer of voices, whether as a young lad in a rectory garden hearing "a voice that's speaking in the wind," the "lin-lan-lone" of the voice from "Far—Far—Away," or the voices of affirmation and denial in 1833. Seventeen years later, those same voices could be distinctly heard, and so it was to the end. Doubt perplexes, faith languishes, the image ("The Two Voices") or the vision (*In Memoriam*, XCV) intervenes, feeling supersedes thought, and faith is guardedly expressed, but the final summation is not victory but precarious and agonized tension.

The oft-noted tension between nature poetry and didactic verse may be illustrated by two poems, one written in 1863 and the other, first published in 1889 but mentioned in "To Mary Boyle" as having been written "more than half a hundred years" before. The former is Tennyson's poem in praise of John Milton. Making an "experiment in quantity" in the style of Alcaeus,[57] he begins the sixteen-line poem eulogistically:

> O mighty-mouthed inventor of harmonies,
> O skilled to sing of Time or Eternity,
> God-gifted organ-voice of England,
>   Milton, a name to resound for ages;
> Whose Titan angels, Gabriel, Abdiel,
> Starred from Jehovah's gorgeous armories,
>   Tower, as the deep-domed empyrean
>   Rings to the roar of an angel onset!

In the first half of the poem adjectives are used which evoke images of massiveness, grandeur, and Titanic stature. Then with a quick side-glance of self-reference, the poet breaks in abruptly with a new subject—himself:

> Me rather all that bowery loneliness,
> The brooks of Eden mazily murmuring,
>   And bloom profuse and cedar arches
>   Charm, as a wanderer out in ocean,
> Where some refulgent sunset of India
> Streams o'er a rich ambrosial ocean isle,
>   And crimson-hued the stately palm-woods
>   Whisper in odorous heights of even.

In this second half of the poem Tennyson uses such key words as "loneliness," "murmuring," "profuse," "charm," "wanderer," "sunset," "ambrosial," "whisper." The imagery has suffered a sea change from the "angel onset" in the "deep-domed empyrean" as described by "mighty-mouthed" Milton, to a quiet, crimson-hued sunset above the whispering palms of some Pacific isle. The transition might be informally paraphrased, thus: Great Milton wrote about the War in

[57] Iambic penthimemerus:

1. $\cup - \cup - \times // - \cup\cup - / \cup -$
2. $\cup - \cup - \times // - \cup\cup - / \cup -$
3. $\cup - \cup - \times // - \cup - \cup$
4. $- \cup\cup / - \cup\cup / - \cup - \cup$

Courtesy of Dr. Rowland P. Graeber, Professor of Greek, Syracuse University.

Heaven in words suggesting action in vastness; but if I were writing about the period of Creation, I would describe the quiet, slow sounds of evening drowsing amidst the lush flora of Eden.

This is an example of Tennyson's conscious self-limitation by comparison with a poet whom he admired. It is not an invidious comparison which says the first is good and the second bad, but it certainly does say that one is large and the other small, that the first roars and the second murmurs. Here the poet is classifying his own poetic focus on description of natural beauty through comparison with a poetic predecessor who was interested in the vastness of space-time and eternal theological issues.

The paradox of the poem on Milton becomes apparent when balanced with another poem. If "Milton" seems to say— I am a nature poet, forsaking all larger issues of life—we must look at a nature poem like "The Progress of Spring," written twenty-four years before and published twenty-five years after. This latter poem traces the "ground-flame of the crocus," as Spring "slides hither o'er the Southern sea," "across" the poet's "garden." But even the

> ample presence of a Queen
> Bountiful, beautiful, apparell'd gay,
> Whose mantle, every shade of glancing green,
> Flies back in fragrant breezes to display
> A tunic white as May! [lines 61–65]

does not wholly satisfy this nature poet. Spring must also have a didactic function to perform in the lives of men:

> I too would teach the man
> Beyond the darker hour to see the bright . . .
> [lines 86–87]

The poet urges men to learn the lesson of Spring's "gradual process":

> That after many changes may succeed
> Life which is Life indeed. [lines 116–117]

The issue which these two poems raise is also the issue the critics raise. In "Milton" Tennyson seems to say: I will write primarily about natural beauty and leave other, larger issues alone. Whereas in "The Progress of Spring," his actual performance would indicate: Even when I write a nature poem I cannot resist reference to my consuming interest in war and peace, death and immortality.

The brief analyses of the tensions exhibited by these five poems stretching across thirty-three years of composition and sixty-nine years of publication are introductory to the more detailed examination of five major tensions in Alfred Tennyson's poetry, as indicated by the titles of the first five chapters of this study: I, Art versus Society; II, Sense versus Soul; III, Doubt versus Faith; IV, Past versus Present; V, Delicacy versus Strength.

I

Art versus Society

Tennyson pondered long and hard upon the competing claims of art and the social order. The first fruits of this silent debate appeared under the title "The Palace of Art," published in *Poems, 1833* (actually issued December, 1832). The first edition contained an introduction to the poem which was omitted in the 1842 version; but the poet's intention was unmistakable even without an introduction which called it a "sort of allegory."

In the first thirty-eight quatrains, the poet "built" his "soul a lordly pleasure-house" (line 1) with four courts upon "a huge crag-platform," (line 4), golden dragon-fountains, gilded galleries, a view of mountain, sea, and sand. The rooms were hung with tapestries portraying hunting scenes, a storm at sea, a rural landscape, a mother and child, Saint Cecilia at the organ, the Islamic paradise, and Uther Pendragon's vale of Avalon—so uninhibited was the eclecticism of Victorian taste. There were portraits of Milton, Shakespeare, Dante, and Homer, and mosaics of the cycles of human life. There were bells in the tower and a golden throne in the great hall. The Soul had made gods of beauty and culture, and itself a god "'holding no form of creed, / But contemplating all.'" (lines 211–212). When the individual soul sees itself as godlike, and other souls as "darkening droves of swine" (line 199), the end is in sight. For three years the poet's Soul enjoyed the Palace, "throve and prospered," but

> on the fourth she fell
> Like Herod, when the shout was in his ears,
> Struck thro' with pangs of hell.
>
> [lines 218–220]

Loneliness, hallucinations, and decay attacked the Soul. After a year of such solitary misery, the Soul

> threw her royal robes away.
> "Make me a cottage in the vale," she said,
> "Where I may mourn and pray."
>
> [lines 290–292]

And the Palace? It was not razed, but it stood waiting until the Soul should "'perchance . . . return with others there / When I have purged my guilt.'" (lines 295–296).

Throughout the introduction and the body of the poem, words are used expressing guilt: "sinful soul," "flowering weeds," "howling in outer darkness," "scorn of herself," "exiled from eternal God," "lost," "all alone in crime," "on fire within," "my sin," "mourn and pray," "purged my guilt." Of what is the Soul guilty? The first stanza suggests an obvious but incomplete answer:

> I built my soul a lordly pleasure-house
> Wherein at ease for aye to dwell.
> I said, "O Soul, make merry and carouse,
> Dear soul, for all is well." [lines 1–4]

This is very innocent and intellectual "carousing": the enjoyment of beauty of mind, form, music, and word. The real crime is indicated later in the poem: "'And let the world have peace or wars, / 'Tis one to me.'" (lines 182–183). The Soul is guilty of solitude, of withdrawal from the human predicament, and of that Satanic pride which permitted a mere mortal to feel "Lord over Nature, lord of the visible earth, / Lord of the senses five." (lines 179–180).

In 1951, Joyce Green wrote about the "explicitly allegorical 'Palace of Art.' In this poem, as is well known, Tennyson renounced artistic self-sufficiency, and declared that the pursuit of beauty must be allied to humility, piety, and social responsibility if it is not to corrupt the soul.".[1] The allegory is

---

[1] Joyce Green, "Tennyson's Development During the 'Ten Years' Silence' (1832–1842)," *PMLA*, LVI (1951), 665.

indeed "explicit," but the imagery and mood are highly complex. A study of the text reveals the joy with which the poet built, the luxuriance of his fancy and the exhilaration with which he "loads every rift with ore." This Palace is no clay pigeon tossed into the air to be shot down by a virtuous social conscience. It is an enduring work of poetic art, and, "so lightly, beautifully built," it must be permitted to stand. The allegory does not sing quite what it seems to say. It is a necessity for any poet to build upon the inspiration of all the memorable dead; he must retreat to halls of dreamlike perfection, but he must also see that this is not the abiding place of the Soul. She—(the Soul is always referred to in the poem as feminine in gender)—may leave in penitence, but she hopes some day to return. The reader cannot help noting the difference in intensity between the joyful, exuberant building of the Palace and the thin penitence of the cottage of mourning and prayer. Cleanth Brooks suggests that "The Palace of Art" showed the sort of poem Tennyson wrote as a substitute for a genuine synthesis of the duties a man owes his art and his contemporaries. He points out that the poem first indulges the reader in all the luxury of ivory-tower escapism, but at the end, as an edifying moral, brings him to a recognition of the immorality of such an attitude.[2] Thus the two claims confront each other, but they are not unified.

We might well expect passages equal in length and richness of imagery describing the social tasks to which the penitent's hand is now set. The Soul has repented and left the Palace; now what will she do? In answer, there is just one quatrain, moving from crag to valley, from Palace to cottage—a solution which sounds as suspiciously solitary as the crime. As Frank Laurence Lucas states: "'The Palace of Art' exchanges one retirement for another, an ivory tower for an ivory cottage 'where I may mourn and pray.'"[3]

[2] Cleanth Brooks, *Modern Poetry and the Tradition* (Chapel Hill, 1939), p. 240.

[3] Frank Laurence Lucas, *Tennyson* (London, 1957), p. 19.

The Palace itself is never destroyed as a thing without value or, worse, a lure of sense. It is permitted to stand and wait until the sin-purged occupant may some day return with companions to share its shining halls and its cultured way of life. It is too simple to say that the moral of the allegory is that a poet must leave his solitary fancy and go to work with his talents in the world of men. That was the contemporary interpretation of Tennyson's friend James Spedding, in the *Edinburgh Review*:

The "Palace of Art" represents allegorically the condition of a mind which in the love of beauty and the triumphant consciousness of knowledge and intellectual supremacy, in the intense enjoyment of its own power and glory, has lost sight of its relation to man and to God. . . . The sin of self-absolution from human cares and duties, finds its appropriate retribution in the despair which the sense of being cut off from human sympathy, when it once forces itself on the mind, inevitably brings . . . the concluding stanzas (as conveying the moral, and especially as showing that it is not the enjoyment, but the *selfish* enjoyment, of her intellectual supremacy—not the gifts, but the gifts as divorced from charity—which he holds to be sinful) must find a place.[4]

The inequality of enthusiasm and number of lines devoted to selfish pleasure on the one hand, and social concern on the other, suggests that the poet is torn between two abiding poles of artistic integrity: to live in seclusion amidst the best and finest that men have thought and made, or to go out into the world carrying there the gospel of beauty and social usefulness. And it is significant to note that the second pole of tension, although indicated as the conclusion of the allegory, is barely sketched, not carved in the round. Fifty-five stanzas for the Palace, one stanza for the cottage; the balance reminds us of the one hundred and thirty-three stanzas for the voice of despair and the five stanzas for the voice of hope in "The Two Voices."

[4] James Spedding, "Mr. Tennyson's Poems, A Review," *The Edinburgh Review*, LXXVII (1843), 203-204.

We know that for Tennyson the question of the social responsibility of the poet was an enduring problem. All through his
career some poems announce a reasoned intention to participate in the world's work while others reveal a yearning for
aesthetic detachment. . . . But one can usually find in Tennyson's work a counterstatement to every unequivocal description
of the nature of poetry. At times the opposing viewpoint is
expressed didactically, as in "The Palace of Art" and "The
Poet", but on other occasions it involves a reversal of the values
attached to a familiar image. The opposition between the
symbolism of *The Hesperides* and the later poem, "Move
Eastward, Happy Earth," illustrates this second process.[5]

"The Lady of Shalott" was first published in 1832 and
virtually rewritten for the 1842 edition. Once again, as in "The
Palace of Art," we find the creative artist in seclusion.[6] On an
island in a river stand four gray walls and four gray towers;
within, the Lady weaves "a magic web with colors gay." No
one has ever seen her look out the casement of her chamber;
to no passerby has she ever waved her hand. So long as she is
content to weave and see the shadows of the world in a mirror
that hangs before her, all is well. Should she ever turn from
mirror to object, from loom to life, she would evoke a curse—
the curse of reality, which has the power to kill the dreamer by
destroying the dream. But she is not content: "I am half sick
of shadows!" Sir Lancelot passes by, the Lady takes three
steps from loom to window, she looks directly upon the outside
world, the web floats away, the mirror cracks, the curse
descends. Dressed all in white, she floats, singing and dying
down the river to Camelot and the world of men and the life
she will never share.

> A gleaming shape she floated by,
> Dead-pale between the houses high,
> Silent into Camelot. [lines 156–158]

[5] G. Robert Stange, "Tennyson's Garden of Art, A Study of 'The
Hesperides,'" in John Killham (ed.), *Critical Essays on the Poetry of Tennyson*
(London, 1960), p. 105.

[6] Green, "Tennyson's Development," p. 666.

The mirror of reflection is broken. The web of retreat is torn. She is no longer a mere spectator of life, "but her entry into active reality takes only the passive form of floating dead down a river in a boat." [7] W. D. Paden notes that "the musical voyage of death that crops up in 'The Dying Swan,' 'The Lady of Shalott,' and the 'Morte d'Arthur' is discussed at length by Faber [George Stanky Faber, *The Origin of Pagan Idolatry*, 1816] who relates these tales to the ancient mysteries. . . ." [8]

Two interior involvements in this lyrically beautiful, mournful poem may be noted. First, there is a play upon the words and ideas of life and death. The Lady is alive in the living death of isolated Shalott, where she lives amidst creative activity and reflections from the living objects outside. But such security cannot be permitted by a poet with a social conscience.   Tennyson himself stated that the climax of the poem was reached when "the newborn love for something, for someone in the wide world from which she has been so long excluded, takes her out of the region of shadows into that of realities." [9] But when she leaves the loom and takes three short steps toward life and love, drawn by the power of sex, she floats down the river of life, singing her own dirge, and dies before she reaches the city of men. Paden points out that Tennyson made this same connection between desire and death in "The Lover's Tale," written when he was only nineteen, and again in "The Ballad of Oriana," published when the poet was twenty-one. [10] Which, for Tennyson, represented real life: Shalott or Camelot? The question is made even more complex because he had reversed the well-known Platonic

[7] Lucas, *Tennyson*, p. 21.

[8] William Doremus Paden, *Tennyson in Egypt: A Study of the Imagery in His Earlier Work* (Lawrence, Kansas, 1922), p. 155.

[9] Hallam, Lord Tennyson, *Alfred, Lord Tennyson: A Memoir by His Son* (New York, 1897), I, 116–117.

[10] Paden, *Tennyson in Egypt*, pp. 89–90.

and Baconian figures of the cave so that the source of reflection is not the ideal but the phenomenal world. Perhaps the phrase Tennyson used in his brief elegy on his friend Brookfield, in 1869, is the closest we can get to his complete meaning— "Σκιᾶς ὄναρ—dream of a shadow." It is not so much the case of this or that, but of categories having some of the characteristics of reality and at the same time some of the characteristics of unreality. Tension has dissolved into ambiguity.

The second, and more important, implication appears if this poem is considered in some limited sense a sequel to "The Palace of Art." What became of the artist who built so splendidly and then left his edifice to mourn and pray? Would the poet's Soul have paid the same final price as the Lady? They both leave isolation and a dream-world. They both are lured out of hiding by concern for others—love for one man, or that love for all men which is born of hatred of the solitary self. When we expect to read what should come next, the description of the redeemed life of social usefulness and participation in man's struggles, the poet's inspiration fails and we are left with a mourning Soul and a dying Lady. Without pushing the resemblance too far, we can say that there is certainly an area of doubt in the author's mind about the meditative versus the active life, the dream versus the deed.

Joyce Green draws an effective connection between the Prologue of "The Palace of Art" and the inscription on the golden fruit in "Oenone." "This inscription ('Oenone'—'For the most fair') directly invites a false isolation of one element in that balanced alliance of beauty, goodness, knowledge, and love, upon which Tennyson had insisted in the Prologue to the 'Palace of Art.'" [11] This comment is doubly interesting since it does not suggest that Tennyson swings pendulum-like from one extreme of isolation to some other extreme of social duty, but that he seeks to hold in consciousness several poles of

[11] Green, "Tennyson's Development," pp. 667–668.

attraction simultaneously—in this case, beauty, goodness, knowledge, and love. The great recipe for living, Tennyson implies, is not the choice of one quality, but that precise and precarious balancing which keeps all four in equal attraction and influence.

Also in the volume of 1832, there appeared the famous tone poem "The Lotos-Eaters." In the Ninth Book of Homer's *Odyssey*, Odysseus brought his men safely past the land of the lotos-eaters by binding them to their places in the boat. The imagery was essentially active, a violent breaking away from the temptation to stasis. Tennyson chose from the tale the theme of stasis itself. He painted a supremely attractive and artistic landscape where ". . . like a downward smoke, the slender stream / Along the cliff to fall and pause and fall did seem" (lines 8–9). It would be impossible to imagine a prosody more in tune and visual line with its object than Tennyson's description of the land of many streams and the yawning accents of the "mild-eyed melancholy lotos-eaters." Robert Preyer points out that as an "oracular poet," Tennyson often wrote a hieratic verse in which "the condition of success depends on a radical distancing and obliquity in the references to human actualities, an intense preoccupation with the sensuous qualities of images, an elaborate and sounding verse texture." [12] The enchanted branches with their burden of fruit and flower are extended to each mariner; those who taste will continue to hear their fellows' voices, but thin and far away, for they will be engrossed by an inner music. Some do taste, and it is with these fugitives from life that the poet stays, "always . . . most at home with the unreal," [13] neglecting even to mention the possibility that some may have declined and sailed away, as was actually the case in the Homeric source.

[12] Robert Preyer, "Tennyson as an Oracular Poet," *Modern Philology*, LV (May 1958), 245.

[13] Hugh I'Anson Fausset, *Tennyson: A Modern Portrait* (London, 1923), p. 31.

And sweet it was to dream of Fatherland,
Of child, and wife, and slave; but evermore
Most weary seemed the sea, weary the oar,
Weary the wandering fields of barren foam.
Then someone said, "We will return no more."

[lines 39–43]

Five Spenserian stanzas portray the essential action of sighting the land, describing the scenery, presenting and tasting the fruit. But the heart of the poem, and perhaps of the poet, is not in the action of the introduction; it is in the feelings and moods of those who ate the lotos, as described in the Choric Song of eight stanzas. They remember and they dream, they live amidst great beauty, their speech is whispered and they often smile, but they wander no more. Just as "The Palace of Art," "The Lotos-Eaters" is concerned with a forbidden evasion of reality. The mariners who choose the island-narcotic commit the same sin, in essence, as the self-isolating Soul in the Palace. "Their error again results from a beauty divorced from the hazards and responsibilities of human life." [14]

In any historical frame of reference, these men would be classed as deserters, but nowhere is this explicitly stated in the poem. Nor is it felt in the conviction of guilt that marred the peace of the Palace of Art. "On one side of his nature, Tennyson would have been well content to be a 'landscape-lover, lord of language,' serving mankind through the delight of images and melodies; but like Keats he was torn between the 'philosopher' and the 'versifying pet lamb,' between Ulysses and the lotos-eaters. His Soul would gladly luxuriate in 'The Palace of Art,' yet she cannot do so without feeling like 'a glorious devil.'" [15] But in "The Lotos-Eaters," by contrast with the world of toil and sorrow, the bitter struggles, the "blight and famine, plague and earthquake . . . clanging

[14] Green, "Tennyson's Development," p. 668.
[15] Hoxie Neale Fairchild, *Religious Trends in English Poetry: 1830–1880* (New York, 1957), IV, 104.

fights and flaming towns, and sinking ships, and praying hands,"
the fugitive mariners seem to have made a very good choice.
At least there is no pain in their withdrawal from life, and no
repentance for fancied or real sin. Although Tennyson left the
fugitive mariners without an expressed social corrective, he
could be confident that his Victorian audience would themselves
supply the criticism and judge them guilty of evasion of duty.

Again we face the fascinating dualism in the mind of the
poet. He has read an archetypal story of travel. He has battled
with the Greeks, in his reader's imagination, through the ebb
and flow of war and storm. Longing for rest, the poet's
imagination pounces upon this tiny incident, which provides
the ancient mariners as well as the nineteenth-century poet
with an almost fatal retreat, and expands it into a full-length
tone poem. Ignoring the opportunity to portray the active life
of the *Odyssey*, he chooses instead to describe the sensuous,
sprawling rest. Of course, as creator, he has the right to portray
mild, melancholy young Greeks in "The Lotos-Eaters" and
vigorous, adventurous older Greeks in "Ulysses"; but this is a
strange game to play with youth and old age, and as the
muscular, active sailors become mild-eyed, melancholy lotos-
eaters, they add one more document to the file of that deep-
rooted tension in the poet's mind—the active or the passive,
the day of action or the long cool evening of withdrawal?

A very early poem, "The Kraken," published in 1830, makes
death the final retreat, rather than the sleep of "The Lotos-
Eaters." The "thunders of the upper deep" die away in the
"uninvaded sleep" of the abysmal depths. Noise and motion
are left behind. But when, in the last days, the kraken shall rise
to the surface again, it will be to roar and die. "We begin with
an active troubled surface motion and proceed directly into a
distanced, quiet, dreamlike stasis. The abrupt transition between worlds is controlled and drawn out in a series of contrasts,
slowed further by repetitions and parallel statements, and almost
brought to a standstill as actions dissolve into antitheses." [16]

[16] Preyer, "Tennyson as an Oracular Poet," p. 241.

The great test of the strength of the poet's will to retreat came in the early eighteen-thirties.[17] In 1831 the Reverend Dr. Tennyson died; the boys' grandfather pressed them hard to take holy orders; Alfred came down from Cambridge with substantial debts but without a degree. In 1832 Christopher North published a mildly critical review of *Poems, Chiefly Lyrical* in *Blackwood's Magazine*.[18] Alfred's favorite brother Charles became an opium addict, and another brother, Edward, suffered a mental breakdown. In April of 1833, Tennyson was brutally attacked by John Wilson Croker in the *Quarterly Review*, and then came the greatest blow of all, on September 15, when Arthur Henry Hallam died suddenly in Vienna of a ruptured blood vessel. As Preyer says of this decade:

No simple explanation can do justice to the complexity of the personal and cultural tensions which he experienced in the decade beginning in 1832. The madness of his brother Edward (committed in 1832), the dope addiction of his brother Charles, the death of Arthur Hallam (1833), and the loss of his patrimony in 1840 certainly exacted an emotional price. He had failed to prepare himself for a job or to gain any real hearing for his poetry. He was convinced he was going blind. Under such stress it was no wonder that he should begin to doubt—and to discount—the apprehensive powers of his mind. In any event, he turned to the writing of mundane domestic idylls and conversation pieces; and he added elaborate and belittling explanations to a number of early poems when they reappeared in the collected edition of 1842.[19]

All of these experiences left their mark, but in the poet's inner life none deserves to be classed with the loss of Hallam. Arthur was more than a friend to Alfred; he was the balance

[17] Charles B. L. Tennyson, *Alfred Tennyson* (New York, 1949), chapters X–XIII.

[18] Edgar Finley Shannon, Jr., *Tennyson and the Reviewers* (Cambridge, Mass., 1952), pp. 7 ff.

[19] Preyer, "Tennyson as an Oracular Poet," p. 251.

that saved him from eccentricity and melancholia, his vital contact with the world, the other needed half of Tennyson's personality, without which he was left in "this widowed state." "Hallam intimately understood Tennyson's delicate sensibility, his basic diffidence, his deep self-consciousness . . . in Hallam's untimely death, Tennyson experienced not only the shattering impact of a profoundly personal loss but also the sharpest reminder of an all-possessing mortality."[20]

Tennyson felt that shattering impact for the rest of his life. But his specific response to Hallam's death was enshrined in the one hundred and thirty-two lyrics of the great elegy, *In Memoriam, A. H. H.*, written with almost incredible constancy across seventeen years, and somewhat reluctantly shared with the world in 1850. Tepidly reviewed by the critics, it was received by monarch and people with tremendous enthusiasm. Samuel C. Burchell speaks of the great influence of the elegy in the Victorian era:

. . . It was a summation of the Victorian temperament and in its period of renown is said to have "rivalled Holy Writ in use and usefulness to Anglican and Evangelical clergymen." Not long before his death Archbishop Benson wrote that the poem was "inexpressibly dear to me for the best part of my life. It came out just when my mother and Harriet died. I sank into it and rose with it, and I used to teach—to love it." For the average Victorian the poem was the great affirmation, a record of the triumphant journey of the soul from despair to faith, a treatise that "gathered up all the doubts of Christianity, of providence, of immortality, which the advance of science had implanted in anxious minds, and answered them or seemed to answer them, with the assurance of a pantheistic and yet personal faith in progress."[21]

The orthodox found in it a vindication of faith. The liberal and scientific read it as a significant prefiguring of evolutionary

[20] Jerome Hamilton Buckley, *The Victorian Temper: A Study in Literary Culture* (Cambridge, Mass., 1951), pp. 74–75.

[21] Samuel C. Burchell, "Tennyson's Dark Night," *South Atlantic Quarterly*, LIV (1955), 75.

thought, since Charles Darwin's *The Origin of Species* was not published until nine years later, in 1859. By its large general public and the widowed Queen it was read as the triumph of faith over despair, but perhaps this was not the reading of the poet himself. He reminded the reader of the poet's right to choose a *persona* other than his own, thus making all autobiographical interpretation hypothetical: "It must be remembered that this is a poem, *not* an actual biography. . . . It was meant to be a kind of *Divina Commedia*, ending with happiness. . . . The different moods of sorrow as in a drama are dramatically given, and my conviction that fear, doubts and suffering will find answer and relief only through Faith in a God of Love. I is not always the author speaking of himself, but the voice of the human race speaking though him." [22]

In such a statement we find the suggestion of several levels of interpretation. There is first the level of the actual event: the death of Arthur Henry Hallam. Second, there is Alfred Tennyson's personal response of sorrow. Third, there is the level of poetic expression which sets forth the event in the terms of image, thought, language, and feeling which will create literary beauty. Fourth, there is any mask the poet chooses to wear, so that the mood and characters of the poem are projected beyond the initial event, making it hazardous to give a wholly autobiographical interpretation. Finally there is the further projection of considering this sorrow in its poetic dress as somehow representative of the sorrows of all men everywhere. By whatever level we approach the poem, we are left with the conviction that the ostensible resolution of conflict by faith is not so strong or so determinative as the resolution of sorrow through the ministry of beauty of word and thought. Hallam noted this resolution in a highly eulogistic analysis of "The Ballad of Oriana." "The strong musical delight prevails over every painful feeling and mingles them all in its deep swell until they attain a composure of exalted sorrow, a mood in which the latest repose of agitation becomes visible, and the

[22] Tennyson (Hallam), *Memoir*, I, 304–305.

influence of beauty spreads like light over the surface of the mind." [23]

It is true that many of the more dramatic poetic passages have to do with doubt rather than faith, but in this chapter, the greater interest lies in the response of the artist to the brutal blow and the slow-healing wound. (The balance of doubt and faith will be treated in Chapter III.) Does this loss lead him to reject God completely or to affirm complete and unwavering faith in immortality? The answer, of course, is neither. The essential role of the artist is neither to reject nor to triumph, but simply to take the gift of sorrow and clothe it in beauty. This process of encysting pain is another evidence of the self-conscious Tennysonian tendency to retreat from event and personal anguish into creative beauty, feeling guilty as he does so:

> I sometimes hold it half a sin
>   To put in words the grief I feel;
>   For words, like Nature, half reveal
> And half conceal the Soul within.
>
> But, for the unquiet heart and brain,
>   A use in measured language lies;
>   A sad mechanic exercise,
> Like dull narcotics, numbing pain.
>   [V, lines 1–8].

F. L. Lucas commented thus upon sorrow clothed in beauty: "When Andromache, Hecuba, and Helen lament above Hector dead, the bitterness of death may seem to grow bitterer still; and yet there is consolation in the beauty of their poetry. And again, as Aristotle saw, the very violence of the grief aroused may leave behind it the calm of passion spent. So with the lamentations of the Muses, age after age, over human life itself. The hideousness of the face of fate may seem half redeemed by the nobility of the faces that confront it.

[23] T. H. Vail Motter (ed.), *The Writings of Arthur Hallam* (New York, 1943), p. 195.

And among those mourning Muses no mean place belongs to Tennyson . . ." [24]

The same play of ambivalence we observed between life and death in "The Lady of Shalott," or between dream and deed in "The Lotos-Eaters," or between self and others in "The Palace of Art," is to be seen here between doubt and faith and the ugliness of human life and the beauty of the poetry about it. Fixed positions shift; tensions remain. "He achieved neither the grace of faith nor the courage of agnosticism. Finally, for Tennyson in *In Memoriam*, God must exist simply because the heart feels an instinctive need of Him." [25]

Sorrow, oblivion, death itself can become acceptable retreats for aesthetic withdrawal. The poems "Mariana" (1830) and "Mariana in the South" (1833) both portray heroines pining, lonely and forsaken, waiting for what they know will not come—"He will not come"—and ultimately for death. "When characters appear in these poems (Oenone, Mariana, the Lady of Shalott, Oriana, and the like) they are likely to be feminine and to utter repetitive apostrophes to nobody in particular." [26] For if "he" did come, it would spoil everything. The glory of the poems is the remarkable evocation of the mood of self-indulgent melancholy, overripe and decadent, yet still beautiful. One may sense that these forsaken women, living amidst "blackest moss" and "blacken'd waters," are, in a perverse way, comforted by the beauty of decaying nature and the melody of their own monotonic sorrow. The "solution" of death looms large in such poems as "Sea Dreams," "Tithonus," *Enoch Arden*, *Aylmer's Field*. Robert Preyer reminds us that "what is offered in these poems [of the 1830's] is comfort and reassurance, a changeless, remote, and detached peace. Now the condition for such 'peace' is the elimination or distancing of violence, fear, and terror." [27] Robert Langbaum,

[24] Lucas, *Tennyson*, p. 19.
[25] Sir Harold Nicolson, *Tennyson: Aspects of His Life, Character and Poetry* (Boston, 1922), p. 269.
[26] Preyer, "Tennyson as an Oracular Poet," p. 243.　　[27] *Ibid.*, p. 244.

in *The Poetry of Experience*, notes the same "longing . . . for oblivion" in Tennyson's poetry. "Most characteristic of Tennyson is a certain life-weariness, a longing for rest through oblivion . . . a subconscious longing for oblivion not as a first step toward the vision of transformed being (Keats' 'Nightingale'), but an end in itself . . . over-richness of land-scape, imagery and cadence that mark it as poisonous though at the same time heady and irresistible wine." [28]

In "The Poet's Mind," the youthful bard of 1830 postulates an isolation of the poet and the inability of a cynical worldling to share his vision which much later he was to rebuke in *In Memoriam* (1850), CVIII: "I will not shut me from my kind . . . I'll rather take what fruit may be / Of sorrow under human skies," and in 1860 in "Tithonus":

> Why should a man desire in any way
> To vary from the kindly race of men,
> Or pass beyond the goal of ordinance
> Where all should pause, as is most meet for all?
> [lines 28–31]

In "The Poet's Mind" he says, quite unashamedly: I go where you cannot go, where my presence brings forth new life, and your presence would destroy. And in "The Poet's Song" (1842), he re-emphasizes the isolation of the creative artist as he walks in the "rain," "outside the town," to a "lonely place." But eight years later in the great elegy, and eighteen years later in the classical poem he underlines the importance for even the poet to identify himself with "the kindly race of men." The correction is not simply a matter of date—the poet has felt the pull of both positions all his years.

Up until this point in the chapter, poems have been considered which, while they reveal the tension between art and society, tilt more toward the aesthetic and away from the social. From this point on, the poems are those which are generally picked by critics to demonstrate Tennyson's social

[28] Robert Langbaum, *The Poetry of Experience* (London, 1957), p. 88.

concerns. *The Princess*, written in 1847, was snorted at by his friendly critic FitzGerald as an example of Tennyson's "old fault of talking big on a common matter." [29] A year later his opinion had not changed and the long poem seemed to him "a wretched waste of power at a time of life when a man ought to be doing his best; and I feel almost hopeless about Alfred now." [30] Today, *The Princess* is cheerfully forgotten except for its incidental songs. Yet the sub-title of John Killham's book—*Tennyson and "The Princess": Reflections of an Age* [31]—remind us that it was one of Tennyson's attempts to be relevant to the issues of his time. The "question of woman," now settled politically but personally and economically as much a question as ever, was in the Victorian era pressing hard upon the minds of thinking men. Long story-poems on love and marriage were being produced by Arthur Hugh Clough—*The Bothie of Tober-na-Vuolich* (1848); Coventry Patmore—*The Angel in the House* (1854–1862); and Elizabeth Barrett Browning—*Aurora Leigh* (1857). The young visitor to Locksley Hall, in the 1842 poem of that name, had spoken of woman as "the lesser man." This was not the last statement Tennyson had to make, through a poetic character or in person, about woman's place in the "chain of being."

In *The Princess*, Tennyson was attempting to sketch out the lines of a new type of relationship. We can be certain that he was aware of the Socialist theories which were undermining conventional attitudes to marriage, and when we have all the facts, it is not possible to regard his attitude toward marriage in the poem as a piece of unthinking conservatism. He shows himself too bold a speculator for that. He was trying to show that even the most advanced of women should not reject legal marriage, as some were tempted to do, because there were

[29] A. McKinley Terhune, *Life of Edward FitzGerald* (New Haven, 1947), p. 126.

[30] *Ibid.*, p. 126.

[31] John Killham, *Tennyson and "The Princess": Reflections of an Age* (London, 1958).

reasons for its continuance; and he sought a wide audience because he believed his reasons deserved it. . . .[32]

In all good conscience, the poet started to write about a social issue. The Prologue opens on a strange mingling of "two nations": the working men attending a Mechanics' Institute who are the heirs to the future, and Sir Walter Vivian's other guests, his son's undergraduate friends, who are the heirs of the past. But the poem quickly slips away from the strained setting of mechanics on the lawn and Cantabrigians on the terrace into an even stranger mythical land of intellectual Amazons and their efforts to be free of men, sex, and marriage. Princess Ida's University for Women was walled, manless, and childless. The young prince who loves the princess can enter this woman's world only by donning woman's garments. He is, of course, discovered, and his kingly father proceeds with his own solution of the woman question—aggressive, masculine force. Two mandalic [33] experiences solve the emotional conflict: the sight of the hero hurt and needing nursing, and the warm cuddling of a little child in bed. Fausset accused Tennyson of being emotionally insincere in introducing episodes to sway his readers to a conventional point of view. But Killham reminds us that Tennyson was not necessarily echoing the opinions of reactionaries who looked on women exclusively as *mères de famille*. If the poem originated in conversations with John Mitchell Kemble about an actually projected university for women, it is even more topical than imaginative. The episodes which arouse Ida's dormant maternal spirit may well have arisen out of the legal suit of Caroline Norton for the custody of her children and the resulting wrangle over the Custody of Infants Bill. [34] Caroline Norton was a very advanced female whose maternal feelings were so strong that she was willing to brave publicity and public

[32] *Ibid.*, p. 4.

[33] "Mandala": Group of Hindu deities enclosed in a circle to indicate relationship. Used by Jung for archetypal relationships, e.g., mother-child.

[34] Killham, *Tennyson and "The Princess,"* p. 173.

opprobrium, and if necessary to change the laws of England, in order that she might keep her children. Again, if this is Tennyson's reference, the pivotal position of the child in *The Princess* is also more topical than sentimental.

Any honest appraisal of the poem would have to recognize that behind the farcical elements and the light opera touches there lies a real earnestness of concern expressed in verse which is, for a social tract, astonishingly lovely. It is illuminating to recall William Paton Ker's linking of *The Princess* and "The Rape of the Lock." "Tennyson's *Princess* is full of things that make it a modern counterpart to the *Rape of the Lock*." [35] Charles F. G. Masterman noted the same similarity when he observed that "what Pope accomplished for the eighteenth century Tennyson effected for the middle period of the nineteenth." [36] Both poets used an elegant style to enunciate those ideas which "oft were thought, but ne'er so well expressed." In *The Princess* Tennyson reproduces Pope's serio-comic touch, the trenchant social criticism made in a bantering manner, and the ambivalence of a mock-heroic which is not so much a mockery of the heroic style as a mockery of men and women who think themselves quite heroic. But entirely Tennyson's is a light earnestness of touch which is almost impossible to simulate. Rather than being shocked by "A Medley," some perceptive contemporary criticism found the conglomerate topic, style and mood quite appropriate to the era. "If a man were to scrutinise the external features of our time, for the purpose of characterising it compendiously, he would be tempted, we suspect, to give up the task before long, and to pronounce the age a Medley. It would be hard to specify the character of our Philosophy, including as it does fragments of all systems, sometimes at open war, and sometimes eclectically combined. In this respect, Mr. Tennyson's

[35] William Paton Ker, *Tennyson*, The Leslie Stephen Lecture (Cambridge, 1909).
[36] Charles F. G. Masterman, *Tennyson as a Religious Teacher* (London, 1900), p. 2.

poem, *The Princess*, not without design if we may judge by the title, resembles the age." [37]

From the point of view of this study, the poem is full of fascinating and unresolved tensions. Killham points out the tension between socialism, positivism, and Saint-Simonism on the one hand, and a conservative view of the position of women on the other. He also suggests a tension in the portrayal of the princess between northern and southern attributes. The immediate impression is that Ida is a kind of medieval heroine, Bradamante and Britomartis rolled into one, tall and quite northern-Amazonian as she strides through her medieval British college close. But a more careful reading reveals her southern, almost oriental attributes. The "Gothic" collegiate courtyard is adorned by "awnings," "a billowing fountain," a "Peacock," "orange thickets," and "meshes of the jasmine and the rose." Ida, herself, has long black hair, wears a jewel on her forehead, and is accompanied by two pet leopards. There is also an odd masculine-feminine ambiguity in the other characters as well as in the Princess. The women not only look and speak like antique warriors, but the men can be admitted only by virtue of close shaves and women's garb. There is also an odd variance between the purpose and the accomplishment of the poet. He obviously intended to write about a contemporary problem and present a modified-liberal solution, but instead, he found himself painting his characteristic picture of female retreat, behind a well-guarded wall, far from men, children, and biology. The inevitable setting recurs: an island in the river, four gray walls and towers, women who have nothing to do with men, but whom, in this instance, the natural touch of a child's caress can restore to reality.

We have noted previously the poet's inability to accept either of two opposing alternatives. In the lyric "Come Down, O Maid" (*The Princess*, VII), the poet cannot accept the high idealistic and intellectual concept held by Princess Ida as the proper position for women. But throughout the poem he has

[37] Aubrey de Vere, in *Edinburgh Review*, XC (July–October 1849), 388.

reiterated that man's world of deed, passion, and materialism is not his proper place either. If woman must come down into the valley of love, fertility, and the common life, man must forsake the lowlands of the commonplace and move up toward the mountains of idealism, thought, and a gentler way of life. One can only hope that in these opposing moves, they yet manage to meet.

The basic solution of "the woman-question" is for Tennyson, characteristically, a tension in opposition. Woman "is not undevelopt man" (Part VII, line 259), nor less than man, but "equal" (VII, line 285) and "diverse" (VII, line 260). In the attraction of diversity lies their individual completion— "either sex alone / Is half itself" (VII, lines 285–286), "each fulfils / Defect in each" (VII, lines 287–288). Their cause is really one, the problem is not the "woman question" but the "man and woman question"—"The woman's cause is man's: they rise or sink / Together" (VII, lines 243–244), "my hopes and thine are one; / Accomplish thou my manhood and thyself." (VII, lines 343–344). And in the evolutionary process, the successful mating of each individual couple contributes to the upward progress of the race—"let us type them now / In our own lives" (VII, lines 283–284). When the factors of equality in diversity, fulfilment in union, and the couple become the race are given their full weight, this does not appear to be an inadequate or dated statement of male-female relationship. And it is a far more melodious armistice of the "war of the sexes" than most:

> O we will walk this world,
> Yoked in all exercise of noble end,
> And so thro' those dark gates across the wild
> That no man knows. Indeed I love thee: come,
> Yield theyself up: my hopes and thine are one;
> Accomplish thou my manhood and thyself.
> [VII, lines 339–344]

"Locksley Hall" and *Locksley Hall Sixty Years After* are important documents in any discussion of Tennyson's social philosophy. The outline of "Locksley Hall," published in 1842, is simple. A young man on a hunting trip finds himself near the home of a young woman he loved and lost. He asks to be left alone until the rest return and summon him with the "bugle-horn." Solitary, he ponders on the familiar landscape and his cousin Amy, who truly loved him but was "puppet to a father's threat" and servile to a mother's "shrewish tongue." She married their choice, who was coarser-fibered than his bride. The hunter conjectures about the disillusionments of her married life and considers that it would have been better for both of them to have died. He curses the social and economic conditions that separated them and asks if it is madness that makes him remember things better forgotten. Amy may some day have a baby to give her solace, but she will rear her daughter as she was reared. He must turn from memory and despair to action. But what can he do? Every door is barred with gold and filled with applicants, and he has only an "angry fancy." So he turns from the unhappy, frustrated present to the distant past, before he was spurned by Amy. He remembers his youthful self-identification with all humanity, his vision of a new world with ships of the air plying commerce and perhaps dropping a "ghastly dew" but issuing into a federated world and a peaceful one beneath the reign of universal law. But the aftermath of his fatal love for Amy has left him suspicious of scientific progress and conscious of a hungry, lionlike people waiting for the old order to die. Sad experience brings knowledge and knowledge leaves behind wisdom, and he will not doubt that some "increasing purpose" runs through all the ages. The horn sounds, his comrades call, he sees his sorrow as they would see it and is ashamed. That woman—"the lesser man"—should have had the power to do this to him! If he could only retreat to that orient where his life began, some isle never visited by ships. There he could marry a native woman and rear a "dusky race." But he rebukes his foolish dream; such a retreat would be a lowering of all he has known, his destiny is in Europe, in his own age, with whatever of promise it may hold. Farewell to Locksley Hall, let it perish since he has now finished with it, carried away on the "mighty wind" of his age.

The only excuse for such a painful analysis is to place Tennyson's social comment firmly within its narrative frame. The frame is present tense; all the comment and criticism are past tense. He loved in the past, was rejected in the past, believed in progress, identified himself with the common herd of men—all in the past. He seeks for action to relieve him from the heartache of the past and the despair of the present and turns to a past further back, when he was more idealistic and had not yet learned the bitter lessons of experience. In the present he considers two possibilities: he might retreat to an island and escape his world, or he might curse Locksley Hall, bury memory, and glide along with the air currents of his era. The former he cannot accept, the latter is all he has left. Like the planet spinning down "the ringing grooves of change," he will go forward, he will change, he will hope his crescent moon has not yet set, and while he cannot strongly affirm it, he will not quite say that he "doubts" the presence of a vital and shaping "purpose" in the world. With this restatement of the mood of the first "Locksley Hall," in which we see far more pessimism than is usually assumed in the neat pattern of "the optimism of the young poet of 'Locksley Hall'" versus "the pessimism of the old poet of *Locksley Hall Sixty Years After*," we turn to the latter poem.

Hoxie Neale Fairchild links the two poems in a relationship with which this study partially agrees. "Probably no one would hesitate to infer that in the two Locksley Hall poems, despite the figment of a story, the poet speaks for himself. If we avoid the common error of supposing that the famous optimistic prophecy in the earlier poem represents the hopes of 1842 rather than a vision of the Cambridge days which the speaker is now vainly trying to recapture, we may say that both poems represent much the same attempt to preserve the obligatory progress-cult in the face of discouragement, but that the pessimism of the later piece is more embittered and querulous." [38]

The second *Locksley Hall*, a dramatic monologue published in 1886 in the volume *Locksley Hall Sixty Years After, Etc.*, takes the chronological reference in the title from the increased age of the speaker of the monologue, not from the difference in publication dates. The young huntsman is now a grandfather who has returned for a funeral to the Hall, which he had promised never to visit again and which he had consigned to rack and ruin. He walks on the seashore and talks to his grandson about Judith, who has just spurned the younger man as Amy had rejected the older long before. But he does not consider the modern case as serious as his own experience had been, although there is much similarity between the lovers' complaints. In the chapel where he once had prayed with Amy, her husband is buried, as is Amy, dead in childbirth, her child, and the crusader ancestor of both their lines. For more than forty years his own wife Edith has been dead, the wife who healed his spirit and "link'd" him again to humanity after Amy had broken the chain. Their sailor son, Leonard, is also dead, leaving only the grandson to whom he speaks. Leonard died a hero's death on a sinking ship, but even his deed is valueless unless men and goodness and truth are "for ever." The grandfather no longer hails human progress as in his earliest youth. Now he recognizes that such progress is enormously slow (aeons of ten thousand years), and as evidence he cites the cruelty of Assyrian kings repeated through the ages by Timur the Mogul, Edward V, religious rivalries, Catholic Rome, the French Revolution, the brutality of Irish peasants—and yet we know, as some of them did not, the teachings and the spirit of Jesus Christ and Saint Francis of Assisi. Who can tell whether human change is from chaos to cosmos or from cosmos to chaos? Hope for the best but remember that the present is the heir of all the bloody past. Was any other age so crammed with menace, madness, written and spoken lies?

[38] Fairchild, *Religious Trends*, IV, 112.

Equality of birth and worth is a myth, and democracy may end by destroying itself. The mob may rush the state into a disastrous war with Russia, yet the peasant or the farmer may have greater natural nobility than the aristocrat or the statesman. The voice of the people may be the ruin of State, Church, and Throne. The frank "naturalism" of artists contributes to the corruption of the young. Ought an old man to be so heated in his criticisms; is he just in his dotage? How can he help being vehement when he remembers his youthful dreams of political justice, the federation of all nations, the abolition of disease by Science, a warless world? The pressure of a mushrooming population will produce wars until this earth is as dead as the moon. Amy still lights up this particular landscape for him as she did at their last meeting sixty years before. Had they known all the carnage and madness to come, they might have wished to dwell on a distant star, or is evil there, too? Evolution climbs toward the ideal, but Reversion drags down toward the mud. The Eighth Psalm, astronomy, and geology question the importance of men, yet God is revealed both in the infinitely small and in the infinitely large. The grandson's train was late because of the vicious prank of a child. Is it progress when mechanical advance is accompanied by the degradation of the workers and their offspring in the cities of England? The youthful grandson must hold to hope and cry "Forward!" with his generation. The old grandfather has lost confidence in his ability to discern the signs of the coming ages. He admits now that Amy's husband was a worthy man; he advises his grandson not to hate his successful rival. Youth and age are small distinctions in the onward sweep of time. The sea-village to which they have walked reveals how "science grows and beauty dwindles." All his friends are "vanish'd voices" and the world is a ghost. In the village inn he had snubbed Amy's husband and now he is full of regret. The grandson might well take the dead squire for an example of life and usefulness. Perhaps, after all, we are led by Powers of good and Powers of ill and the "highest human nature is divine." "Follow light," do right, for man has half-control of his destiny. As he now loves the man he once loathed, he realizes that love conquers at the last. He died at eighty, he who speaks is eighty, and his grandson is now the heir and master of Locksley Hall.

Hallam Tennyson informs us that "my father said that the old man in the second *Locksley Hall* had a stronger faith in God and in human goodness than he had had in his youth; but he had also endeavored to give the moods of despondency which are caused by the decreased energy of life." [39] This statement so annoyed Mr. Fairchild that he replied, "if *Locksley Hall Sixty Years After* is more optimistic than *Locksley Hall*, and seems more pessimistic merely because the senile poet is deliberately trying, as a dramatic experiment, to sound a little senile, one is tempted to throw down one's cards and rise from the table, protesting that it is impossible to play the game of criticism with so slippery a man." [40]

One cannot help sympathizing with Mr. Fairchild's frustration, for in the prose comments on his poetry Tennyson often seems to be trying to elude both the critic and personal responsibility. But the real problem does not arise from Tennyson's parrying of critical thrusts but from the central ambivalence of the poems themselves. In "Locksley Hall" the young man turns from a frustrating and cynical present to a painful and intolerable past. Trying to escape the anguish of memory he turns even further back into the past to a time of youthful idealism. But his attempt to recapture the mood of innocence after he has drunk the fatal potion of experience is hopeless and so he returns hopelessly to a hopeless present. He will live in his age, think and act, but without any great expectation of what may be accomplished. So the poem moves elusively in four tenses: the idealistic past, the painful past, the frustrating present, and the hopeless future. It is difficult to "play the game of criticism" with Tennyson.

[39] Tennyson (Hallam), *Memoir*, II, 329.
[40] Fairchild, *Religious Trends*, IV, 112.

At the beginning of *Locksley Hall Sixty Years After*, the grandfather refuses to identify his experience with Amy with his grandson's experience with Judith. At the close of the poem he is quite ready to forgive and appreciate Amy's husband and to urge his grandson to do the same for Judith's husband. This is not contradiction but simply dramatic development within the mind of the speaker. If the later poem "seems more pessimistic" it is not only because the poet quite justifiably permitted the querulous complaints of old age to creep into the portrait of an old man of eighty, but because we read the former poem incorrectly, attributing the optimism of the Cambridge days, which the huntsman is trying unsuccessfully to recapture, to his state of mind after the loss of Amy. And there is excellent reason to accept Tennyson's statement, which is surprising only on the surface: "the old man . . . had a stronger faith in God and in human goodness." We have already shown, in the discussion of the earlier poem, that all the faith the youth could express was in the negative terms "I do not doubt." In the later poem he states definitely that "That which made us meant us to be mightier by and by" and into the infinitely small universe of the microscope and the infinitely large universe of the telescope, "Sent the shadow of Himself, the boundless, thro' the human soul; / Boundless inward in the atom, boundless outward in the Whole." This is by no means an ultimate pessimism; it far more resembles Carlyle's figure of the universe as the clothing of God. By identifying God with man, atom and universe, it becomes the curious opposite of "The Higher Pantheism": "Earth, these solid stars, this weight of body and limb, / Are they not sign and symbol of thy division from Him?" In *Locksley Hall* they become the "sign and symbol" of union, not division.

The second half of the statement—"faith . . . in human goodness"—is even more defensible. In the early poem, the huntsman turned from betrayal by individuals to humanity and the stirring events of a world in motion. In the later poem, the grandfather turns from the uncertain verdicts of history to appreciation of one he had once hated and reconciliation with the one who had betrayed him. Thus the movement is exactly balanced: from individual to universal, from universal to individual. The young man, disappointed in love, turns to the world for solace. The old man, disappointed in the world, turns to individual loved ones for comfort and hope. In this sense, one may say that "the old man . . . had a stronger faith . . . in human goodness." And his climactic statement, "Love will conquer at the last," is both similar to and more hopeful than the conclusion of Matthew Arnold's "Dover Beach" or the final scene of Archibald MacLeish's *J.B.*

Mr. Gladstone was much disturbed by Tennyson's picture of the present age, and in extenuation he offered the improved postal service, the universal availability of newspapers and the wide activities of Thomas Cook's tourist agency in promoting British travel abroad.[41] But this is a bit like explaining to the Good Samaritan that his activities will no longer be necessary once Rome has thoroughly policed the road from Jerusalem to Jericho. It is not law but humanity with which Tennyson is concerned and which he sees always fallen among thieves of various complexions and on all the roads of history.

The chief difference in tone-color between the two poems comes from the two pictures of the human crowd. In "Locksley Hall" the hunter recalls an earlier visit to London and his eager identification with the throngs of men there—"Men, my brothers, men the workers, ever reaping something new; / That which they have done but earnest of the things that they shall do." But sixty years after the grandfather refers to the rural rick-burnings which were current during the poet's college days:

> peasants maim
> the helpless horse, and drive
> Innocent cattle under thatch, and burn the
> kindlier brutes alive.

41 William Ewart Gladstone, *Nineteenth Century*, XXI (January 1887), 1.

Brutes, the brutes are not your wrongers
—burnt at midnight, found at morn,
Twisted hard in mortal agony with their
offspring, born-unborn

Clinging to the silent mother! Are we
devils? are we men? [lines 94–99]

and points with horror at the effects of city life upon the yeo-
manry of England, "City children soak and blacken soul and
sense in city slime." As for the apothegm *vox populi, vox Dei*, he
refers to the champions of the voice of the people thus: "You
that woo the Voices—tell them 'old experience is a fool,' /
Teach your flatter'd kings that only those who cannot read can
rule" (lines 131–132), a passage highly reminiscent of Shakespeare's *Coriolanus*:

Here come more voices.—
Your voices: for your voices I have fought;
Watch'd for your voices; for your voices bear
Of wounds two dozen odd; battles thrice six
I have seen and heard of; for your voices have
Done many things, some less, some more: your voices.[42]

Indeed, along with his refusal to expect to see progress except
in terms of tens of thousands of years, there runs a Coriolanus-
like disgust with the mob, but without the Roman's pride in
personal integrity—for the old man has learned that he too is
changeable, fickle, and untrustworthy. Of course, the emphasis
upon the necessity of slow progress and great periods of time if
progress is to be noted at all is reminiscent of Edmund Burke's
antirevolutionary, organic theory of social change and of the
political philosophy of William Lamb, Lord Melbourne:
"'Whenever you meddle with these ancient rights and juris-
dictions it appears to me that for the sake of remedying
comparatively insignificant abuses you create new ones and
always produce considerable discontent,' he observed to
someone who proposed reforming the financial administration

[42] William Shakespeare, *Coriolanus*, II, iii, 132.

of the Duchy of Cornwall. 'Delay' and 'postpone' were still his favourite words if any political project was under discussion." [43] Back in 1833, in the poem "Love Thou Thy land, with love Far-Brought," the poet had expressed his suspicion that extended suffrage meant the emergence of the professional politician, not widened democracy:

> But pamper not a hasty time,
>   Nor feed with crude imaginings
>   The herd, wild hearts and feeble wings
> That every sophister can lime. [lines 8–11]

In the same poem he had expressed his belief in change that came naturally, in "its season":

> Not clinging to some ancient saw,
>   Not master'd by some modern term,
>   Not swift nor slow to change, but firm;
> And in its season bring the law, [lines 29–32]

and in "You Ask Me, Why, Tho' Ill at Ease," of the same year:

> Where Freedom slowly broadens down
> From precedent to precedent;
>
> Where faction seldom gathers head,
>   But, by degrees to fullness wrought,
>   The strength of some diffusive thought
> Hath time and space to work and spread.
>   [lines 11–16]

The references to these early poems do not simply reinforce the statement of Tennyson's Burkean political philosophy in *Locksley Hall Sixty Years After*. They also remind us that this was not a development of old age. The fact that Tennyson held approximately the same views about progress when he was a young poet as when he was old can best be indicated by a characteristically balanced statement of 1846. In "The Golden Year" Tennyson quotes a poem by "Leonard" (who was called a "tongue-tied poet in the feverous days," perhaps a reference to criticisms leveled at Tennyson's aestheticism) in

[43] Lord David Cecil, *Melbourne* (New York, 1954), p. 347.

which the fictitious poet speaks of the slow movement of progress—"And slow and sure comes up the golden year." Then choleric James, like Moses breaking his staff upon the rock, heatedly replies, "well I know / That unto him who works, and feels he works, / This same grand year is ever at the doors." Here, as in "The Two Voices" and *In Memoriam*, is once again the primacy of feeling—one must not only work, but "feel" that he works. If one were to ask, is Tennyson Leonard or James, the answer would have to be, he admires and perhaps envies James both his certainty and his emphasis upon feeling and doing; but Tennyson is the wistful Leonard. James' "athletic" faith insists that the Golden Year can come the instant men are willing to work for it. Leonard's wistful yearning can only hope it will come some time. The central statement of the later *Locksley Hall*, addressed to the son of another Leonard, is also a message of hope ungirded by certainty and unsubstantiated by history:

> Hope the best, but hold the Present fatal daughter
>   of the Past,
> Shape your heart to front the hour, but dream not
>   that the hour will last. [lines 105–106]

"Cry your 'Forward,'" not because it is necessarily going to happen, but simply because "yours are hope and youth, but I—" Thus the social poems end in the same tension as the elegies of *In Memoriam*. Live and act as if there were social progress and personal immortality, not because you know that they are so, but because you need to believe in them.

In the tension between Art and Society (or between Evolution and Reversion, or Cosmos and Chaos), the tendency to retreat from the world and the corrective return to the world are both clear and ubiquitous. The artist is neither an aesthete betrayed into social conscience nor a prophet of Victorian progress who occasionally doubts his own message. He is a man in whose life and verse the one and the many struggle, and continue to struggle, each for its proper place and meaning.

II

Sense versus Soul

Ever since Jesus said, "Render to Caesar the things that are Caesar's, and to God the things that are God's" [1] men have conjectured on the precise quantity and quality of the division. Not the least of these was Alfred Tennyson. He was celebrated in his day as a poet of faith; in our day he is a poet of doubt. He was sensitive all his life long to the beckoning of beauty and the withdrawal of vision; but he was also sensitive to the civic idealism of his friends and the pressing needs of his generation. The luminescence of spirit suffuses his poetry with its mingled light and gloom; but he could see "the moon reflected in a nightingale's eye." [2] "This young man comes and tells me that ash buds are black; and I look, and they *are* black." [3] He is a romantic and an idealist and a sentimentalist; but he is also a realist, a Classicist and a satirist. As much as any man he struggled to render both to Caesar and to God and was most often rent himself in the lacerating division.

Jude the Obscure attests to the fact that Tennyson's war between "sense" and "soul" was not unique in the Victorian era. "Hardy defines Jude's struggle as a 'constant internal warfare between flesh and spirit.' . . . Hardy, like his older contemporary Tennyson who wrote in the *Idylls of the King* about 'sense at war with soul,' constantly redefines his problem and re-orients his theme." [4]

[1] The Gospel According to Mark, XII, 17.

[2] Frank Laurence Lucas, *Tennyson* (London, 1957), p. 13.

[3] Elisabeth Cleghorne Gaskell, *Cranford* (New York, 1891).

[4] William E. Buckler, Introduction, Thomas Hardy, *Jude the Obscure* (New York, 1959), p. 8.

In his two-volume memoir of his father, Hallam Tennyson reported an experience which the poet called "a kind of waking trance, I have frequently had, quite up from boyhood, when I have been all alone."[5] Alfred Tennyson ascribed a similar experience to Sir Galahad, in the poem by that name first published in 1842.

> And, stricken by an angel's hand,
>   This mortal armor that I wear,
> This weight and size, this heart and eyes,
>   Are touch'd, are turn'd to finest air.
>   [lines 69–72]

In "The Holy Grail," first published in 1869, the poet attributed the experience to King Arthur:

> and many a time they come,
> Until this earth he walks on seems not earth,
> This air that smites his forehead is not air
> But vision—yea, his very hand and foot—
> In moments when he feels he cannot die,
> And knows himself no vision to himself,
> Nor the high God a vision, nor that One
> Who rose again. [lines 907–914]

It is apparent, in both of these poems, that the poet is writing about two orders of reality with which he is intimately acquainted: "this earth" and that which "seems not earth," "this air" and that which is "not air / But vision."

Chapter I of this study examined the tendency of the poet to retreat into aestheticism—not as a stage or a final position in the development of his poetic genius but always within the magnetic field of a counterattraction that drew him back into the world, there to face those problems of the meaning of human life and relationship and death that haunted him always. This chapter examines the poetic evidences that Tennyson was deeply concerned about the basic nature of

[5] Hallam, Lord Tennyson, *Alfred, Lord Tennyson: A Memoir by His Son* (New York, 1897), I, 330.

reality—was the real stuff of the world matter or spirit, dream or awakening, vision or deed, theology or morality, this world or that hypothetical world to come? Aestheticism provides the withdrawn artist with a temple of beauty in which he may exult in the treasures of the past, the glories of the natural universe in the present, and the plan of continued self-cultivation in the arts for the future. Asceticism, on the other hand, presents to the saint fleeing from the world a citadel of the spirit where he may deny all the tawdry glories of the world he has known in the past, cultivate his own spiritual nature in the present and prepare for Heaven, his soul's true home, in the future. Both aestheticism and asceticism bear the obvious resemblance that they are retreats. They offer the fugitive soul a hiding place from the challenges and demands common to the daily lives of ordinary men. Tennyson affirmed and denied the validity and reality of both the aesthetic retreat and the social return. The same ambiguity, dubiety and ambivalence are operative in his treatment of soul and sense.

The discussion of aestheticism led to the recognition of it as one complementary pole of tension, with the active life as the other pole. In the examination of the competing demands of the world and the spirit, the polarity of tension is just as marked, for the poet not only describes with great skill and power the attractiveness of the mystic vision and the ascetic quest; he also explicitly presents a contradictory and remedial this-worldliness.

"Sir Galahad," from which some quotation has already been made, designates in its first lines the dual themes of the poem: "My strength is as the strength of ten, / Because my heart is pure." These are the twin topics of the total poem: physical strength and usefulness coupled with spiritual purity and other-worldliness. The next lines tell of the ladies who love the young knight, but to whom he does not give his heart, for he is completely devoted to the spiritual exercises described in lines seventeen to twenty-four. Then for forty-three lines the two worlds are drawn together. The knight sees the light of a stormy new moon, but sees as well a supernatural light which "swims, / Between dark stems," making the forest glow. In the natural stillness of the wood, he hears "a noise of hymns." Standing by a real mountain lake, he again superimposes vision upon physical reality:

> I find a magic bark,
> I leap on board; no helmsman steers;
> I float till all is dark. [lines 38–40]

Lines sixty-nine to seventy-two describe the trance experience quoted at the beginning of this section, and the next seven lines reveal a transfigured knight and a voice from heaven: "'O just and faithful knight of God! / Ride on! the prize is near.'" The closing four lines bring the knight back to earth again. He is in the world but not of the world; he rides across material fields, securely clad in shining armor, not looking for maidens and dragons but for the Grail and that moment when "down dark tides the glory slides, / And starlike mingles with the stars."

Even this brief analysis makes clear the composition of the poem as it shuttles back and forth with marvelous dexterity between the "ten-man-knight" pole of jousts and maidens, and the pole of visionary transfiguration. If the precise balance were to be sought, it would certainly lean toward the vision and away from the maidens and the jousts.

A poem written when Tennyson was eighty and included in the 1889 volume underlines the importance of spirit and the transiency of flesh. In "Happy: The Leper's Bride" the poet is playing his old game of the juxtaposition of opposing titles— "Forlorn" just precedes "Happy"—which have within them an internal paradox. The former is a wild, emotionally heightened poem of death and marriage, illegitimacy and confession. A literary ballad, it is both sentimental and tragic. The normal expectation would be to match it with a charming poem of healthy normality. But the "happy" person is the bride of a leper, who sees in leprosy an indictment against all flesh and a vindication of the primacy of spirit. The imagery is as sordid and strong as anything in Browning's "Childe Roland to the Dark Tower Came" or T. S. Eliot's *The Waste Land*.

> body is foul at best.
> The fairest flesh at last is filth on which the worm will
>   feast;
> This poor rib-grated dungeon of the holy human ghost,
>   This house with all its hateful needs no cleaner than the
>   beast,

IX

> This coarse diseaseful creature which in Eden was divine,
>   This Satan-haunted ruin, this little city of sewers,
> This wall of solid flesh that comes between your soul and
>   mine,
>   Will vanish and give place to the beauty that endures,
>   [lines 28, 31–37]

There can be no question that "the beauty that endures" is exalted in the poem. Yet, as has often been noted in Tennyson's writing ("The Palace of Art," *In Memoriam*, etc.), the quality which is judged wanting is the quality that evokes the major poetic interest: the feasting "worm," the "rib-grated dungeon," "this little city of sewers."

In 1888, Alfred Tennyson arranged the twelve books of the *Idylls of the King* to follow the calendar months from Spring and the first meeting of Arthur and Guinevere, to December and that "last weird battle in the West." It was dedicated to Albert, the Royal Consort, and in an *envoi* asked the Queen to "accept this old imperfect tale, / New-old, and shadowing Sense at war with Soul." It seems to me that the three intentions of the poem are indicated in these few words. First, it was an "old imperfect tale." For his source of inspiration, the poet turned from his age back to the Arthurian legends which

John Milton had once considered as a possible basis for his *magnum opus*. By turning to the remote past he incurred Thomas Carlyle's epithets of retreat: "finely elaborated execution," "inward perfection of vacancy," "the lollipops were so superlative," "skillfully wrought of high imaginings, faery spells, fantastic legends, and mediaeval splendours . . . suffused with the Tennysonian glamour of golden mist . . . like a chronicle illuminated by saintly hands," "a refuge from life," "a mediaeval arras" behind which Tennyson fled from "the horrors of the Industrial Revolution." [6]

Carlyle was by no means the only one of Tennyson's friends who criticized him for any diversion from the needs and movements of contemporary social history. The poet was retreating from "the horrors of the Industrial Revolution," but characteristically, he retreats in order to interpret; he steps back in order to clear a space for hurling his lance at the present. For the second notable characteristic of those few words in the *envoi* is that although based upon an old tale, the poem Tennyson wrote was "new-old": old in source but new in relevance, or dealing with qualities so eternal that although old, they are also always new. F. E. D. Priestley pointed out the modern relevance of the *Idylls of the King* in an article in the *University of Toronto Quarterly*:

Tennyson is asserting in the *Idylls* that Christianity is not so much a set of facts to be argued about as a system of principles to be lived by; that the proof of these principles is to be established not by external empirical evidence, but by the power with which they unify and give stability and meaning to the life of men and of societies. He wants to make the reader understand how these principles become neglected, and what must happen to individuals and societies who neglect them. He is voicing a warning to his own age and nation, and to all ages and nations. He is consistently opposing a revival of the Lucretian philosophy with its materialism, its naturalism, and

[6] C. E. Norton (ed.), *The Correspondence of Thomas Carlyle and Ralph Waldo Emerson* (Boston, 1894), II, 339–340.

its secularism. To him it is the philosophy of pessimism and despair, of defeat and social destruction.[7]

The third item to be noted in those two lines from the *envoi* is that the poem is concerned with an epic struggle between "sense" and "soul." This battle gives heroic character and unity to the poems but it is, at the same time, curiously a source of disunity and failure. Because Tennyson keeps redefining each of his terms, and keeps bringing to them the full ambivalence of his tortured poetic vision, we find ourselves admiring sense and deploring soul just as often as the anticipated reverse. Priestley makes a smooth resolution of this ambivalence by establishing a relationship which is partially so, but basically not so:

Tennyson is asserting through the *Idylls* the primacy of the Unseen, the ultimate reality of the Spiritual, which is manifested in a constant succession of phenomena, and gives permanent meaning to them. The phenomena are not merely shadows or illusions; they are "real" in that they are the actualization of the ideal. Man's task is not to pierce through the evil of appearances and brush it aside; it is to recognize the relationship of appearance to an ideal reality which he cannot fully know, and to work in the realm of phenomena towards more complete actualization of the ideal in so far as he knows it.[8]

Priestley is quite correct in pointing out both the primacy and validity of the "Unseen" and the criticism of the spiritual when it does not issue into life and deed. He errs, along with the best of recent critics, in seeming to find a smooth resolution of the conflict between dedication to an ascetic ideal and absorption in a compromised actuality. Both poles are and remain tormentingly real for Tennyson and create a real war of sense with soul, rather than a sham battle meant to indicate that the opposing forces were actually on the same side all the time.

[7] F. E. D. Priestley, "Tennyson's Idylls," in John Killham (ed.), *Critical Essays on the Poetry of Tennyson* (London, 1960), p. 254.

[8] *Ibid.*, p. 251.

In the actual order of publication, the last idyll, "The Passing of Arthur" (that part of it adapted from the "Morte d'Arthur" of 1842), was the first; followed by the third, "The Marriage of Geraint," in 1857; the fourth, "Geraint and Enid," 1857 (these two originally having been one poem); the sixth, "Merlin and Vivien," 1857; the seventh, "Lancelot and Elaine," 1859; the eleventh, "Guinevere," 1859, the order of these five being based upon the 1859 publication arrangement; the first, "The Coming of Arthur," 1869; the eighth, "The Holy Grail," 1869; the ninth, "Pelleas and Ettare," 1869; the twelfth, "The Passing of Arthur," 1869 (the amplification beyond the "Morte d'Arthur"); the last four in the publication order of 1869; the tenth, "The Last Tournament," 1871; the second, "Gareth and Lynette," 1872; and the fifth, "Balin and Balan," 1885.[9] As Edmund Clarence Stedman visualized, "Nave and transept, aisle after aisle, the Gothic minster has extended, until with the addition of a cloister here and a chapel yonder, the structure stands complete."[10]

Tennyson called it "an allegory,"[11] and Priestley adds that it might be considered a dramatic allegory in which the twelve poems are combined into three groups of four each, forming the three acts of a modern play.[12] Act I opens with the symbolism of "The Coming of Arthur" and closes with the materialism of "Geraint and Enid." Each of the idylls included reaches a happy ending as part of the general theme of order established and good triumphant over evil. Gareth gladly accepts his knighthood and Arthur's sovereignty. By overcoming the Star Knights and the Knight of the Castle Perilous, he finds perfect freedom in service and fulfils Arthur's function

---

[9] Richard Jones, *The Growth of the "Idylls of the King"* (Philadelphia, 1895); W. J. Rolfe (ed.), *The Complete Poetical Works of Tennyson* (Boston, 1898), pp. 302–303; George Benjamin Woods and Jerome Hamilton Buckley (eds.), *Poetry of the Victorian Period* (New York, 1955), p. 971.

[10] Edmund Clarence Stedman, *Victorian Poets* (Boston, 1903), p. 175.

[11] Tennyson (Hallam), *Memoir*, II, 443.

[12] Priestley, "Tennyson's Idylls," pp. 252 ff.

in the world of men. Gareth and Lynette are the incarnation
in humanity of the spiritual ideals of the King. Geraint and
Enid are their foils as they stubbornly follow other standards
and are only finally brought to a recognition of the validity of
the Arthurian standard for them. They do not represent the
recalcitrance of positive evil but the normal obstacles that any
ideal must contend with if it is to become effective in the world.
Along with these positive exemplars of the ideal, there are
foreshadowings of the conflict of Act II. The knights are few;
some are lazy and others mean of spirit. Beyond the Camelot
built by magic to music there stretches the wasteland and the
dark and evil North, where Arthur's sovereignty is denied,
his birth called into question and his power only spasmod-
ically effective through the daring of individual knights.
It was a rumor about Guinevere and Lancelot that led
Geraint to suspect Enid. Evil was not only talked about;
it had already influenced the actions and attitudes of others
and begun the spread of social contagion. These elements
moderate the pattern of success in Act I and build the bridge
to Act II.

The second act opens with the grim fratricide of "Balin and
Balan" and closes with the spiritual splendor but the social
deterioration of "The Holy Grail." The love of Lancelot and
Guinevere moves from rumor to hard fact. Merlin's magic is
canceled through his weariness of spirit and senile lust for
Vivien. The futile fumblings of an old man prove capable of
dissolving integrity as easily as the hot blood of youthful
passion. In the tumult of passion and the cynical resignation of
spiritual power, the innocent Elaine is pathetically involved.
Through the sadly mixed motives and the tragically mixed
accomplishments of "The Holy Grail," the Arthur of Act
I, a savior-king with his full table of disciple-knights, is left
the betrayed master of a barren board and a decimated
order.

The last act begins with a bitterly ironic parallel to the
Gareth of the first act. Pelleas also is young, eager and zealous,

but he seeks to please a lady, not a king, by the rules of courtly love to win a mistress rather than the approval of Arthur. He chooses for his ideal the harlot Ettarre, who cares for experience, not innocence. Betrayed by his friend Gawain and his lady Ettarre, the disillusioned knight turns against Arthur and the vows of knighthood he had taken, for the impact of betrayal was not only social, but it nibbled away at the dwindling fund of the ideal. In "The Last Tournament," which the poem renames "The Tournament of the Dead Innocence," Tristram, who repudiates everything the Round Table stands for, wins the prize for which he does not care and presents it to Isolt, who does not want it, just before he is stabbed from behind by her husband, King Mark. The fool Dagonet is Arthur's only defender as the ideal is seen to be folly when unrelated to human life. The repentant Guinevere in the cloister at Almsbury ponders on the dead values she valued too late as Arthur sets off for a battle which is already lost, in defense of a kingdom which is a hollow form ready to collapse upon its own emptiness. In "The Passing of Arthur" the melancholy gloom of the decease of the highest and best is relieved by the cosmic perspective in which each victory and each defeat is seen as only one small scene in an eternal drama in which the Spirit of God seeks to incarnate Himself in the world of flesh in all ages, in varying ways.

Books I–VII and Book VIII present two important and opposite disintegrating factors. In the first seven idylls the secret love of Lancelot and Guinevere is the disintegrating force which splits the Table Round, destroys the kingdom, and undermines the king. In Book VIII the Holy Grail is the disintegrating factor, representing as it does religious fervor coupled with consequent social evasion. As Jacob Korg points out, "it seems clear that the waning of Arthur's power has as its condition the disappearance of Merlin, and as its main causes the adulterous love of Guinevere and Lancelot and the disastrous effect of the Grail Quest upon the fellowship of the

Round Table." [13] Merlin is the mediating figure between the Grail, which draws men away from life, and Guinevere-Lancelot, whose physical passion blots out the ideal. Merlin, unlike Arthur, has the power to use his magic to create a real city, in other words, to make the unseen seen, to clothe the noumenal with the phenomenal. Perhaps this is the link between the Merlin of the *Idylls* and the wizard who tutors the poet in "Merlin and the Gleam."

Book VIII, "The Holy Grail," is of sufficient importance to justify a somewhat closer analysis than the other books of the *Idylls of the King*. It was based upon Books XIII–XVII of Sir Thomas Malory's *Morte d'Arthur*. Malory, in the second half of the fifteenth century, wrote at the end of Book XVII, "this story of the Sancgreal, that was brevely drawen oute of Frensshe in to Englysshe. . . ." This statement of source probably refers particularly to the French prose *Lancelot*, but may incorporate other more distant ancestors in the late thirteenth-century *Quest of the Holy Grail*, and the twelfth-century *Conte du Gréal* of Chrétien de Troyes. The neglect of Malory as Tennyson's source may well be one of the pitfalls of Tennyson scholarship, for "The Holy Grail" is so full of the latter poet's characteristic muted melancholy and deep sense of decay and death that the unwary reader immediately credits Tennyson with the mood and manner of treatment. But a rereading of Malory points to the opposite conclusion. Tennyson's Arthur hears of the quest and the vows of his knights in his absence, and:

> his face
> Darken'd, as I have seen it more than once . . .
>
> "Woe is me, my knights," he cried,
> "Had I been here, ye had not sworn the vow."
>
> ". . . one hath seen, and all the blind will see.
> Go, since your vows are sacred, being made.

[13] Jacob Korg, "The Pattern of Fatality in Tennyson's Poetry," *Victorian Newsletter*, XIV (Fall, 1958), 10.

> Yet,—for ye know the cries of all my realm
> Pass thro' this hall—how often, O my knights,
> Your places being vacant at my side,
> This chance of noble deeds will come and go
> Unchallenged, while ye follow wandering fires
> Lost in the quagmire! Many of you, yea most,
> Return no more."
>
> [lines 272–273, 275–276, 313–321]

In Malory:

. . . Alas, said King Arthur unto Sir Gawaine, ye have nigh slain me with the avow and promise that ye have made; for through you ye have bereft me the fairest fellowship and the truest of knighthood that ever were seen together in any realm of the world; for when they depart from hence I am sure they shall never meet more in this world, for they shall die many in the quest. And so it forthinketh me a little, for I have loved them as well as my life, wherefore it shall grieve me right sore, the departition of this fellowship. . . .[14]

Like Tennyson's Grail, Malory's *Gréal* glows red and is covered with white samite. The *Gréal* has some functions not shared by the Grail. On several occasions it feeds the knights with all manner of delicious viands. It also has the power of healing, mentioned on at least three occasions. For both authors, the quest is not for sinful man. Thus Lancelot is barred from the clear sight of the Grail. Malory makes this requirement very specific: the knights are not to be accompanied by women; virginity is even more desirable than chastity; the knights carry holy emblems, eat no meat, drink no wine, attend Mass daily. Tennyson takes the figure of Percivale's sister from Malory, but makes her more central to the appearance and meaning of the Grail. Malory has only half of the knights who set out on the quest return; Tennyson raises the fatality rate and brings back only a tenth. Malory makes Galahad king of the city-state of Sarras and follows his coronation by reception of the

[14] Sir Thomas Malory, *Morte d'Arthur* (London, 1889). Thomas Wright (ed.), Book XIII, Chapter VII, 620.

Gréal at the hands of Joseph of Arimathea, death, and ascension. Tennyson has no death but a magnificent, Wagnerian fiery apotheosis and kingship in that "far off country." Both writers make Percivale a hermit holy man until his speedily subsequent death.

Thus instead of taking a lusty and vigorous romance and covering it with the muted shades of melancholy, Tennyson found his source material already beautifully suited to his purpose and characteristic mood. He deals basically with a problem of incarnation—how a spirit can take on the trappings of sense, be clothed in flesh, take a wife, call knights to the standard of pure conduct and social helpfulness, and establish the Kingdom of God on this green earth. "Ideal manhood closed in real man" is caught in a war between "Sense" and "Soul," in a time "that hover'd between war and wantonness." Guinevere and Lancelot are the malefactors of Sense. They corrupt the Table from within, destroy the king's confidence in men, and disillusion the chastity of the maiden knights. Thus, unwillingly and therefore tragically, they represent Sense and are its "typical wrong-doers." Samuel Burchell points out the literary family relationships of Tennyson's picture of the later Round Table. "The progress from fruitfulness to decay is seen most clearly in the last five of Tennyson's idylls, where Arthur's kingdom has become an arid land full of disloyalty and adultery and lack of faith. Here the once radiant Knights of the Round Table are revealed as ugly and selfish and without honor—with souls as empty as those Eliot found in the hollow men or Conrad saw at the innermost station of the heart of darkness."[15] Sir Harold Nicolson noted this same resemblance to Eliot's *Waste Land*.[16]

But if Tennyson makes Lancelot and Guinevere the malefactors of Sense, he makes the Holy Grail the malefactor of

[15] Samuel C. Burchell, "Tennyson's 'Allegory in the Distance,'" *PMLA*, LXVIII (1953), 422.

[16] Sir Harold Nicolson, *Tennyson: Aspects of His Life, Character and Poetry* (Boston, 1922), p. 334.

Soul—and at this point we see once again his underlying ambivalence and his own most trenchant criticism of the retreat into asceticism. He insists that both symbols represent kinds of excess: the first that excessive physical passion which ought to be consummated in marriage and the birth of children, if it has any place at all.   In his drama *Queen Mary*, published in 1875, Tennyson makes clear that with many gifts of loyalty and devotion, it was Mary's excessive passion for Philip that destroyed her reign.

> MARY: . . . Gardiner is against him;
> The Council, people, Parliament against him;
> But I will have him! My hard father hated me;
> My brother rather hated me than loved;
> My sister cowers and hates me. Holy Virgin,
> Plead with thy blessed Son; grant me my prayer.
> Give me my Philip; and we two will lead
> The living waters of the Faith again
> Back thro' their widow'd channel here, and watch
> The parch'd banks rolling incense, as of old,
> To heaven, and kindled with the palms of Christ!
>   [I, v, lines 51–61]

Mary's lawful passion as effectively blocks her social usefulness as Guinevere's illicit passion makes her a bad queen.

But the Grail is likewise an excess: a fanatical other-worldliness that blinds men to social responsibilities, to worthy covenants already sealed. It is the Grail which decimates the Round Table, breaks the quasi-religious vows to the Priest-King Arthur, and finally wrecks the Christian State.

Alfred Tennyson set up a similar pair of heroes in "The Vision of Sin" and "St. Simeon Stylites," both published in 1842. The adulterers and the pilgrims of the Grail quest are matched by the sinner and the martyr of the two briefer poems, for both cut themselves off from the world of men, although the means for one is self-indulgence and for the other, calculated renunciation. In "The Holy Grail," the Victorian poet forcefully indicates that not only is there the problem of a pair of illicit lovers who count all the laws and duties of the world slight things in comparison with an overwhelming physical passion; there is also the problem of knights who count all the world well lost for God. Thus Tennyson examines the symbol of the Grail, recognizes its clamant power over the spirits of men, but rejects its asceticism by showing what it did to Arthur's state, and, by implication, what the retreat into asceticism would do to any individual or state.

Thus far this discussion has included only the three chief characters of the *Idylls of the King*: Arthur, Guinevere, and Lancelot. In the crucial eighth idyll, already analyzed in terms of symbolism, each character responds in an individual and significant way to the Holy Grail, and it is worthwhile to note these reactions somewhat in detail. Galahad and Percivale's sister, both virginal, are the persons everyone agrees are holy enough to see the Grail. The sister-nun is disturbed by her clear recognition that the world about her is inhabited by an "adulterous race." Having seen the Grail, she desires to bring it to the sight of others in order that "all the world be healed." Thus in her "public life" she unites vision and social ideal, but in her private life she represents a withdrawal from active participation in life, love, and marriage. Does Tennyson mean her to be admired, deplored, or, more probably, both? Galahad, the nun's male counterpart, receives the sword-belt woven of her hair and forces the appearance of the Grail by sitting deliberately in the Siege Perilous, there "to lose himself that he might be saved." He does see the Grail, and is translated to the far-off country where he will become a king. Stopford Brooke affirmed that this apotheosis was "done as no one has done this kind of work since Dante." [17]

> A thousand piers ran into the great Sea.
> And Galahad fled along them bridge by bridge,
> And every bridge as quickly as he crost
> Sprang into fire and vanish'd, tho' I yearn'd

[17] Stopford A. Brooke, *Tennyson: His Art and Relation to Modern Life* (New York, 1899), p. 327.

To follow; and thrice above him all the heavens
Open'd and blazed with thunder such as seem'd
Shoutings of all the sons of God. And first
At once I saw him far on the great Sea,
In silver-shining armor starry-clear;
And o'er his head the Holy Vessel hung
Clothed in white samite or a luminous cloud.

And when the heavens open'd and blazed again
Roaring, I saw him like a silver star—

And o'er his head the Holy Vessel hung
Redder than any rose, a joy to me,
For now I knew the veil had been withdrawn.

[lines 503–513, 516–517, 520–522]

Again the question arises: Galahad had daring, purity and perseverance, but was the direction of his life-dedication a wholly admirable one? Bridges that vanish bear no commerce of man or trade, and kings of far-off countries can scarcely also be responsible citizens of the land they left behind.

Gawain settles down in the first comfortable berth he finds along the way. Sir Bors would willingly give up the vision which he receives in order that Lancelot might see. Lancelot is aware of two growths in his soul: the flower of friendship for his king-comrade, and the weed of adulterous love for that comrade's wife. He seeks the Grail that the latter growth might be rooted out. He sees the Grail, but "veil'd and covered," amidst a fiery hell. The poet implies that the vision is enough to rebuke sin, but not enough to purify and transform. Lancelot is wounded by the sight of purity, but he is not given the gift of purity.

Percivale, the teller of the tale to the monk Ambrosius, is the real center of the narrative. On his lonely quest, he sees all the things that would have to be given up for the sake of the Grail: the pleasures of the senses, the love of wife and child, wealth and splendor, fame and glory—and finally his own self lost to save himself, just as Galahad had expressed it. When he sees the Grail, it is as a shared vision through witnessing the

blood-red apotheosis of Galahad. Ambrosius' responses to
Percivale's story, which is told in heroic style, are delightfully
earthbound. After hearing about the glory of Galahad, the
flaming bridges, and the shouting sons of God, he mutters to
himself: "Rejoice, small man, in this small world of mine,"
and counts the blessings of mingling with common folk,
hearing the gossip of old wives and the mirthful sayings of
children "that have no meaning half a league away." And
when the knight tells how he denied his boyhood sweetheart
for the sake of his vow, the monk replies,

> O the pity
> To find thine own first love once more—to hold,
> Hold her a wealthy bride within thine arms,
> Or all but hold, and then—cast her aside,
> Foregoing all her sweetness, like a weed!
>
> [lines 619–623]

He congratulates himself once more that he is "content to sit
by little fires." Of course all this is a beautiful foil to parry the
thrust of the noble Grail Quest, and moreover it expresses
Tennyson's own recognition that such idealism is open to
ridicule. It is a deep-rooted ambivalence which makes a monk
affirm the claims of quiet fires, comfortable villages, wealthy
brides, sexual love—all based on a broken vow—and a knight
affirm the unrelenting claim of the ideal.

The most surprising reaction is the king's. Arthur is a kind
of soul seeking incarnation in the world. Tennyson stated:
"My meaning in the *Idylls of the King* was spiritual . . . Arthur
was allegorical to me. I intended to represent him as the ideal
of the soul of man coming into contact with the warring
elements of the flesh." [18] The King dwells in a palace conjured
up for him by Merlin, with carved zones showing four stages
of human progress: men being killed by beasts, men killing

---

[18] Hallam, Lord Tennyson (ed.), *Works of Alfred, Lord Tennyson* (New
York, 1908), II, 443 n. Annotated by the author.

beasts, warriors fighting each other, and men growing wings. Surely the Quest for the Holy Grail would be most suitable for men who are meant to become angels and grow wings. But Arthur's face darkens when he hears of the Quest:

> "Woe is me, my knights," he cried,
> "Had I been here, ye had not sworn the vow."
>   [lines 275–276]

Then with much realism and even brutal frankness for a man of soul, he tells them they are not capable of succeeding in such a quest. For Galahad, for the nun, and for Percivale, yes; but the rest are strong men in battles and blind men in spiritual matters. When a few knights return to a dilapidated hall in a storm-wrecked city, he reminds them grimly:

> '"Was I too dark a prophet when I said
> To those who went upon the Holy Quest,
> That most of them would follow wandering fires,
> Lost in a quagmire?—lost to me and gone,
> And left me gazing at a barren board,
> And a lean Order. . . ."' [lines 885–890]

Then he remembers that Percivale had said that had the king been present at the first invitation of the Grail, he too would have forsaken all to follow. Now Arthur rebukes him with the disciplined responsibility of a ruler:

> the King must guard
> That which he rules, and is but as the hind
> To whom a space of land is given to plow,
> Who may not wander from the allotted field
> Before his work be done. . . . [lines 901–905]

But when that work is done, then he may dream dreams and see visions "until this earth he walks on seems not earth." This delicate balancing of responsibilities to heaven and to earth is quite different from the case of "Ulysses," who sails off so gloriously, "beyond the utmost bound of human thought," and leaves his son Telemachus

> to fulfill
> This labor, by slow prudence to make mild
> A rugged people, and through soft degrees
> Subdue them to the useful and the good.
> Most blameless is he, centered in the sphere
> Of common duties. . . . [lines 35–40]

Both Arthur and Ulysses make it clear that they think there are men made to see and follow visions and men meant to bear earthly responsibilities. "'St. Agnes' and 'St. Simeon Stylites,' together with 'Sir Galahad,' probably written a few months later, suggest that religious asceticism, though permissible to some minds, is fraught with danger for others: a St. Agnes finds satisfaction; a St. Simeon wastes life and deludes himself and others." [19]

Yet such a division into mystics and worldlings is too simple. Arthur is by nature a visionary, but his responsibilities keep him chained to a disintegrating kingdom until his task is done. Thus he must be both a man of earth and a man of heaven. This is the measure of Tennyson's failure with Arthur: as man of heaven he is an effective symbol, but his incarnation into humanity is never quite complete or successful. He is not human enough to be a satisfactory husband or an understanding comrade of men. The king who blames his knights for impetuous dedication to visionary quest is himself a visionary.

The poet painted, with extraordinary beauty and pathos, a kingdom in which ideally men were to evolve from beasts to angels, but where men were actually torn between the social challenge of righting this world's wrongs and their sworn oath to follow the gleam of a heavenly Grail. When ascetic retreat is clamant upon the spirits of men, it is impossible either to deny

[19] Joyce Green, "Tennyson's Development During the 'Ten Years' Silence' (1832–1842)," *PMLA*, LXVI (1951), 671.

or to satisfy. It is just as the old Seer warned Gareth in "Gareth and Lynette,"

> the King
> Will bind thee by such vows as is a shame
> A man should not be bound by, yet the which
> No man can keep. . . . [lines 265–268]

Robert Langbaum refers to·this pattern, reversed, in "St. Simeon Stylites": "it is St. Simeon's hatred of life and blurred vision of people at the base of his pillar that accounts for his vividly hallucinatory vision of the angel offering a heavenly crown, and that leads us to perceive in that hallucination the bursting forth of his deepest desire, the meaning of his whole life and thus of the poem."[20] The hallucinatory vision is not the fruit of the love of God, but of the hatred of men. In "The Holy Grail" Tennyson turns the tension in the other direction. Arthur's knights hear the high call and thus are forced to neglect the demands of ordinary duty. Simeon turns deliberately away from the life of men and thus has a vision—received or self-induced, the poet leaves it to us to decide. Whichever it may be, it is clear that vision, in both poems, is shown as the foe of the common tasks of life: Percivale a hermit and Simeon on a pillar. It is by no accident that the poet accompanied the first appearance of the Grail with "'A cracking and riving of the roofs, / And rending, and a blast, and overhead / Thunder and in the thunder was a cry'" (lines 183–185).

Among the several verse plays written by the Laureate with such extraordinary and unrewarded persistence, *Becket* was published in 1884. The basic, historic fact with which the play deals is the assassination of Thomas à Becket at Canterbury. The play provides one more illustration of Tennyson's tension between the retreat of asceticism and the thrust of civic duty.

The creative problems of the dramatist in dealing with this actual event lie in the areas of character and motive, since the action is already set. In the Prologue, Becket, already Chancellor, receives word that he is to become Archbishop of

[20] Robert Langbaum, *The Poetry of Experience* (London, 1957), p. 208.

Canterbury as well. Immediately, in Act I, Scene i, the king's favorite resolves that he "'shall go against'" the king and along "'with the Church'" (line 54). Twenty-nine lines later he muses, "this Canterbury is only less than Rome." In the third scene of the same act, he is accused by a disappointed rival of being so "bolster'd up with stubbornness and pride" that in fighting for the Church he may destroy it (line 18). In Act V, Scene ii, John of Salisbury, his friend and "conscience," warns him that his unwillingness to forgive the Bishop of London and the Archbishop of York may be interpreted as "mixing our spites / And private hates with our defence of Heaven" (lines 26–27). In the same scene, he notes in an aside, "How the good Archbishop reddens! / He never yet could brook the note of scorn" (lines 158–159). In the following scene he doubly rebukes Becket: "Is strength less strong hand-in-hand with grace?" and "My Lord, I marvel why you never lean / On any man's advising but your own" (lines 298, 300–301). Self-sufficiency and proud integrity are the keynotes of character that both friends and foes observe in this Tennysonian portrait of the great archbishop.

Becket's motivation of escape from intolerable tensions by death is established early in the play and is a recurring motif thereafter. In the first scene of the first act, Becket cries, "I am martyr in myself already" (line 200). Two scenes later he refers again specifically to martyrdom (iii, line 105). In the same scene, he implies that his martyrdom "begins at the top" rather than upside down as tradition describes the martyrdom of Peter (line 352). The next scene speaks of his blood "poured out upon earth" and "mounting to heaven" (line 33). In Act IV, Scene i, Walter Map warns that further moves of the archbishop against the king may draw him toward death in his defense of the Church. Becket, in exaltation, replies, "to die for it—I live to die for it, / I die to live for it" (line 254). In the fifth act and second scene, the same John of Salisbury admonishes, "will *you* drown *yourself*? / He loses half the meed of martyrdom / Who will be martyr when he might escape" (lines 147–149). With far greater penetration than he dreams, the assassin, De Brito, delivering the final blow, mutters: "This last to rid thee of a world of brawls" (V, iii, line 104). The reader's mind goes back to a juvenile poem, the "Ode to Memory" from the 1830 volume, in which the artist addresses memory:

> Artist-like,
> Ever retiring thou dost gaze
> On the prime labor of thine early days,
>   retired
> From brawling storms. . . .
>
>   [lines 92–94, 111–112]

The early poem affirms the artist's need of withdrawal, perhaps to recollect emotion in tranquility. The late play permits the main character the ultimate limit of the ascetic retreat from "a world of brawls"—death, which might have been avoided, but from the beginning of the play is foreshadowed as the dénouement.

In 1935, when T. S. Eliot prepared a play on the same historic event, having "read" Tennyson's "before setting to work on his own play,"[21] he used the same central motif of pride of spirit. Eliot's four Tempters offer what is essentially one temptation: memory of the past joy of life and the proud insistence that it can come again, pride in past political accomplishments, pride of birth and nationality, and last, pride in spiritual integrity.[22] Eliot's Becket realizes that although all the tempters appeal to pride, the fourth temptation is the "greatest treason," to "do the right deed" (defend the Church) "for the wrong reason" (in order to force assassination and ultimate sainthood).

John Peter points out the same ambivalence in Tennyson's play. "If on the one hand Becket is proud and wilful then he is no martyr, and his death is merely a personal downfall with no significantly religious implications. If on the other hand he

---

[21] John Peter, "*Murder in the Cathedral*," *Sewanee Review*, LXI (1953), 365.
[22] T. S. Eliot, *Complete Poems and Plays* (New York, 1952), pp. 183–191.

is a saint, it is fatal, or at least absurd, to represent him as impetuous and headstrong, constantly requiring the restraining admonitions of John of Salisbury, plainly his superior in most respects." [23] It may be "fatal," but it is not "absurd" to anyone who recognizes what Tennyson was about. If he is presenting the high dream of a man caught in impossible tensions in his active life, that man might well come, in his interior life, to the conclusion that death would be both a defense of his duty and the only possible resolution of tensions.

Although both playwrights choose the central theme of spiritual pride, there is a most revealing difference in characterization. Eliot's Becket is a strong man confronting a strong king and defeating him from the grave. Never is there any shakiness of the hand, any sense of inadequacy to meet either the day by day problems of his bishopric or the final decision that must be made. Tennyson's Becket is a good man, a well-intentioned and stubborn man, but essentially a weary one. It is easy to sense his great relief as he retreats from the practical concerns of life via the eternal peace of martyrdom. The Chancellor-Archbishop of Tennyson's drama does not really get murdered; he absconds. Here is the very essence of Tennyson's problem. When the Grail led Percivale into a monastic life, leaving his place vacant at the Round Table, Tennyson seems to be unable to decide whether this is the spiritual progress men are supposed to be making, or a kind of desertion. The monk Percivale chose the clear road of personal spiritual nurture; the knight Percivale would have had to wrestle with the complex compromises involved in righting the world's wrongs. Perhaps God made Becket one of His martyrs; or perhaps the Archbishop simply escaped by death from the impossible tensions of this life: the tension of state versus church, or secular versus sacred, of earthly friendship versus divine loyalty.

As was suggested at the beginning of this chapter, world-negating asceticism is usually focused upon Heaven, making

[23] Peter, "*Murder in the Cathedral*," p. 365.

this world's glories look tawdry and cheap. Thus Galahad sees the sweet glances of ladies and will battle for them "till the end," but as for his dominant allegiance, he says, "all my heart is drawn above." The Quest of the Grail is earth's highest and holiest mission, but it draws Galahad to a far city from which there is no return, makes Percivale a monk and decimates the Arthurian Round Table. When Ulysses follows knowledge "beyond the utmost bound of human thought," he leaves to an "aged wife" and the "slow prudence" of his son Telemachus the practical task of meting justice to a "savage race" among their "barren crags." St. Simeon woos a vision which blots out the people at the foot of his pillar and which, by awarding a heavenly crown, will release him from the life he loathes. Thomas à Becket is slain in his own cathedral, but by that deed, both becomes a saint and is released from "a world of brawls."

However, there is another variety of asceticism which comes not from the hope of the future glory of heaven but from the weight of the recollections of a former ideal existence, making the present sad and incomplete by comparison. In the nineteenth century, William Wordsworth expressed the doctrine of pre-existence in the famous ode:

> Our birth is but a sleep and a forgetting:
> The Soul that rises with us, our life's Star,
>   Hath had elsewhere its setting,
>   And cometh from afar:
>   Not in entire forgetfulness,
>   And not in utter nakedness,
>   But trailing clouds of glory do we come.[24]

In the twentieth century, Thomas Wolfe gave literary expression · to the doctrine in the Prefatory Poem to *Look Homeward, Angel*: "Naked and alone we come into exile. In her dark womb we did not know our mother's face; from the prison of her flesh have we come into the unspeakable and

[24] William Wordsworth, "Ode: Intimations of Immortality from Recollections of Early Childhood."

incommunicable prison of this earth . . . remembering speech-
lessly we seek the great forgotten language, the lost lane-end
into heaven," [25] and again in the autobiographical lines about
the early death of his brother Ben: "Like Apollo, who did his
penance to the high god in the sad house of King Admetus, he
came, a god with broken feet, into the gray hovel of this world.
And he lived here a stranger, trying to recapture the music of
the lost world, trying to recall the great forgotten language,
the lost faces, the stone, the leaf, the door." [26]

Dugald MacEachen finds traces of the same belief in pre-
existence in one of Tennyson's sonnets: "In the sonnet titled
'To ——' in the 'Early Sonnets' in collected editions of
Tennyson, the poet tells a friend that when he met him for the
first time he had the strange feeling that they were already old
and very close friends. The sonnet hints that the explanation
of this psychological phenomenon is a state of pre-existence." [27]

A belief in pre-existence cannot be claimed as a major
strain in the writings of Tennyson, but enough material can
be marshaled to establish it as a minor strain. The importance
and relevance of this minor note are apparent when we recognize that pre-existence is the archetype of all retreats in the
measure that memory is more real than anticipation.

In reference to the early sonnet "To ——" as hinting at the
doctrine of pre-existence, Mr. MacEachen is on solid ground,
as indicated by such lines as:

> As when with downcast eyes we muse and brood,
> And ebb into a former life, or seem
> To lapse far back in some confused dream
> To states of mystical similitude . . .
>   "All this hath been before,
> Methought that I had often met with you,"
>   [lines 1–4, 7, 13]

[25] Thomas Wolfe, *Look Homeward, Angel* (New York, 1929), p. 2.
[26] *Ibid.*, p. 557.
[27] Dugald B. MacEachen, "Tennyson and the Sonnet," *Victorian Newsletter*, XIV (Fall 1958), 6.

Another more famous poem, "The Two Voices," also written by 1833, shoots a "random arrow" from the poet's brain that "old mythologies" may contain some truth. A draught of forgetfulness is drunk as we slip "from state to state," yet: "'So might we, if our state were such / As one before, remember much'" (lines 355–356), and if he had "'lapsed from nobler place,'" "'Some legend of a fallen race / Alone might hint of my disgrace'" (lines 369–370). He vaguely considers the evolutionary theory that he has come up "'thro' lower lives.'" But moving from theoretical alternatives to experience, even though unclear and dreamlike, he affirms that

> 'Moreover, something is or seems,
> That touches me with mystic gleams,
> Like glimpses of forgotten dreams—
>
> 'Of something felt, like something here;
> Of something done, I know not where;
> Such as no language may declare.'
>
> [lines 379–384]

The major argument of the poem was discussed in the Introduction, but the additional affirmation of the poet may be noted that he has experienced a previous, higher life, beyond the power of words to describe. It is only fair to add that not only is this beyond the power of words to describe, but it is also beyond the power of belief for Tennyson to affirm, so that the best he can say is that pre-existence "is or seems"— "like something"—"I know not where."

On August 11, 1852, the poet's first son, Hallam, was born. That same day, Tennyson wrote a double poem "De Profundis: The Two Greetings," which Stopford Brooke called "the finest of his speculative poems. Its stately and majestic sublimity is warmed by the profound emotion of his fatherhood." [28] The second part of the second half of the poem contains reference to birth as a banishment and "lostness" from the previous "true world."

[28] Brooke, *Tennyson*, p. 453.

> O dear Spirit, half-lost
> In thine own shadow and this fleshly sign
> That thou art thou—who wailest being born
> And banish'd into mystery, and the pain
> Of this divisible-indivisible world . . .
>
>   [II, ii, lines 5–9]

Previously he had been writing in rather traditional fashion of the new life coming from "out of the deep" where "God moves as he will." Such a statement is perfectly orthodox, expressing the conventional belief that God fashions each life as in Genesis He fashioned the first man. At the other end of life, Shelley can sing, with complete orthodoxy, that Keats in death "hath awakened from the dream of life." [29] But when Tennyson writes of birth as banishment, he moves quite out of the Judeo-Christian tradition into Greek metaphysics. Incidentally it is a curious gap that Christian theology should maintain complete silence concerning the life of the soul before birth. The implication is that excepting in the case of pre-existence of Jesus, the soul has no prior life, being created some time in the process of fetal maturation.

In the "Prefatory Sonnet to 'The Nineteenth Century,'" 1877, Tennyson asked "If any golden harbor be for men / In seas of Death and sunless gulfs of Doubt." The answer of Christian orthodoxy would be couched in the future tense. But in "The Ancient Sage," published two years earlier, the disillusioned seer has only questions about the future and sees the present world "dark with griefs and graves." It is from the past, the furthest distant past of a prior existence, that he recalls "sweetness" and "love." He speaks first of his boyhood:

>   for oft
> On me, when boy, there came what then I call'd,
> Who knew no books and no philosophies,
> In my boy-phrase, "The Passion of the Past."
>
>   [lines 216–219]

[29] Percy Bysshe Shelley, "Adonais," line 344.

and then of a time preceding even that:

> A breath, a whisper—some divine farewell—
> Desolate sweetness—far and far away—
> What had he loved, what had he lost, the boy?
> I know not, and I speak of what has been.
>
> [lines 225–228]

Such passages establish the biographical connection between the imaginary ancient sage talking about his boyhood and the real poet, who at the age of five cried ecstatically, with arms spread wide in the March storm, "I hear a voice that's speaking in the wind," and over whom the phrase "Far, far away" exercised a strange charm, and who later admitted to his son that the "Passion of the Past" fell upon him as a boy.[30] Indeed for this rectory child, "the tide of time flowed back with me, / The forward-flowing tide of time."[31] It flowed backward not only to the tales of knights and ladies and the golden light that played on Greece, but back, at least on a few occasions, to the "desolate sweetness" of a world he "had lost" by being born into this world.

In the total sweep of Tennyson's thought, this prior world scarcely figures in bulk or importance. But in the discussion of his tendency to withdraw from the struggles of this world into an ideal world of spiritual reality, it does remind us that just as Heaven drew Galahad, Percivale, and St. Simeon forward, so nostalgic recollections of pre-existent glory drew the poet backward in the "Early Sonnets," "The Two Voices," "De Profundis" and "The Ancient Sage."

[30] Tennyson (Hallam), *Memoir*, II, 319.
[31] "Recollections of the Arabian Nights."

III

Doubt versus Faith

"We can look back at *In Memoriam* and poetry of its class as representing a distinct period, standing out sharply bounded as matter for history; which period we may name, from its prevailing tendency, the theological period of nineteenth-century literature. Of that period, represented by such names as Robert Browning, Elizabeth Barrett Browning, Matthew Arnold, and Arthur Hugh Clough, *In Memoriam* is perhaps the most distinguishing monument." [1] Its size, scope of content, and impact on its age unquestionably make it at least a significant work. But any thorough discussion of *In Memoriam* must face three major problems: the exceptionally close male relationship of a pre-Freudian age; the difficulty of making any coherent analysis which clearly reveals the interrelationships of the elegies; the impossibility of arriving at a simple statement of the total meaning and effect of the poem. A consideration of these difficulties is a necessary preliminary to any summation of the elegy's fund of doubt and faith, the impact of science, and the relation of its thought to traditional philosophy.

It is difficult to read *In Memoriam, A. H. H.* (1850) in our Freud-ridden age without sharing the comment of the critic who felt it excessively "amatory"[2] as between males, or the honest confusion of the journalist who wrote: "these touching lines evidently come from the full heart of the widow of a

[1] John F. Genung, *Tennyson's "In Memoriam": Its Purpose and Its Structure* (Boston, 1894), p. 63.
[2] Quoted by Sir Harold Nicolson, *Tennyson: Aspects of His Life, Character and Poetry* (New York, 1922), p. 163.

military man."[3] This is a difficulty which would have received sympathetic understanding from Arthur Henry Hallam himself, as evidenced by his balanced statement of the importance of the emulative love of man for man expressed in Plato's *Phaedrus* and *Symposium*:

Plato saw very early, that to communicate to our nature this noblest kind of love, the love of a worthy object, would have the effect of regeneration to the soul, and would establish conscience in nearly the same intimacy with the world of the senses, which she already maintains with our interior existence. Hence his constant presentation of morality under the aspect of beauty, a practice favored by the language of his country, where from an early period the same Τό καλόν had comprehended them both. Hence that frequent commendation of a more lively sentiment than has existed in other times between man and man, the misunderstanding of which has repelled several from the deep tenderness and splendid imaginations of the Phaedrus and the Symposium, but which was evidently resorted to by Plato, on account of the social prejudices which at that time depressed woman below her natural station, and which even had the philosopher himself entirely surmounted them, would have rendered it perhaps impossible to persuade an Athenian audience that a female mind, especially if restrained within the limits of chastity and modest obedience, could ever possess attractions at all worthy to fix the regard, much less exhaust the capacities of this highest and purest manly love.[4]

Tennyson, a rector's son as well as a classicist, might also have adduced the Old Testament friendship of David and Jonathan, which was "wonderful, passing the love of women."[5]

If sex is defined in Freudian terms, as any extension from the single personality to another personality, then the poem is

---

[3] Hallam, Lord Tennyson, *Alfred, Lord Tennyson: A Memoir by His Son* (New York, 1897), I, 298.

[4] T. H. Vail Motter (ed.), *The Writings of Arthur Hallam* (New York, 1943), p. 158.

[5] II Samuel I, 26.

certainly sexual. But if we think of sexuality in narrower and more customary terms, although we find some physical description of the departed, a few references to embraces, and a sorrow in the survivor that leads to thoughts of self-destruction, there is no hint of an overt homosexuality. Canon Fox's suggestion is helpful in indicating the problem of language involved in such an elegy. "The expression of love between men and women has a conventional language at its disposal, but this language is not admissible between Alfred and Arthur, and therefore not available for *In Memoriam*. Yet *In Memoriam* cannot apparently do without it, because there are no alternatives." [6]

There is every reason to believe that Tennyson—"the virgin spirit in a Titan's form" [7]—recognized his special need of a friend who could give him confidence, lead him out of his dark moods, and balance his recessive temperament with the vigor of normality. ". . . he was rich where I was poor, / And he supplied my want the more / As his unlikeness fitted mine" (LXXIX). Hugh Fausset said that when Tennyson lost Arthur, he "lost not only voice, hand, and face—but the voice of his conscience, the spur to a more virile imagination, that inspiration which might have enabled him to triumph over his weaker nature in the end." [8] In *The Princess*, Tennyson spoke of a person before marriage as half a person, with the marriage partner the other potential half. In *In Memoriam*, he expressed not merely bereavement or loneliness, but the feeling that his loss left less than one full personality. When Virgil, to whom Tennyson has often been compared, went on a voyage, his friend Horace invoked the gods to "preserve the half of myself"—"*Et serves animae dimidium meae.*" (Liber Primus III).

[6] Canon Adam Fox, "Tennyson's Elegy," *Spectator*, CLXXXIV (June 16, 1950), 816–817.

[7] Nicolson, *Tennyson*, p. 57.

[8] Hugh I'Anson Fausset, *Tennyson: A Modern Portrait* (London, 1923), p. 64.

St. Augustine recorded his reaction to the loss of a friend in imagery strikingly similar to Tennyson's in *In Memoriam*:

. . . I was sick of living, yet afraid to die. I suppose that the intensity of my love made death, which has robbed me of him, seem hateful and dreadful, like some horrid enemy; and I thought that it must soon destroy all men because it had slain him. . . . I marvelled that other men should be alive since he was dead whom I loved as if he could never die, and I marvelled still more that I, his other self, should be alive since he was dead. Well did the poet say of his friend: "O thou half of my soul." For I felt that my soul and his had been but one in two bodies; and life seemed horrible to me, because I was cut in two. And perhaps, that is why I feared to die, lest the other half of him whom I had loved so dearly, should perish.[9]

A hint that Tennyson was aware of the problem is found in the sixty-first poem. "I loved thee, Spirit, and love, nor can / The soul of Shakespeare love thee more." This may mean only that even a greater poet, like Shakespeare, could not have loved Arthur more. But more probably it means: As Shakespeare wrote immortal sonnets to a beloved young man, so my poems may be less but my love for Arthur Hallam is as great.

But of course there are striking differences that Tennyson would be the first to wish pointed out. In the *Sonnets* of Shakespeare love is earthly, recognizes the immortality only of the poet's art, languishes in the absence of the loved one and sets no higher goal than union once again. It begins and ends in the privacy of the love of one man for one man. *In Memoriam* moves from personal sorrow to the deep questions of the value of art, the existence of God, the effectiveness of His purpose in the world, and the relationship of the artist to the bereavements and doubts of all men.

Many persons have addressed themselves to the task of writing an analysis of the elegy. Nineteenth-century attempts,

[9] Augustine, *Confessions* (London, 1946), Book IV, Chapter vi, Section 11, p. 58. Translated by E. B. Pusey.

like Genung's and Davidson's,[10] tend to be detailed and to reveal clearly the preconceived bias that Tennyson was a religious teacher and *In Memoriam* a poem of Christian hope and faith. They also show a surprising lack of recognition of Tennyson's wide scientific knowledge and its application to the problems of faith and immortality. Twentieth-century efforts, like Masterman's,[11] Fairchild's,[12] and Buckley's,[13] give up the attempt to make a detailed and interrelated analysis from section to section, and are content to indicate the major trends of philosophic thought. Any honest analysis will have to be somewhat spotty and erratic because these "wild and wandering cries" reveal only the most general outline and refuse to fit any intellectual straitjacket.

Based on the "Christmas Cycles" the elegy falls into five major parts: Introduction I–XXVII; First Cycle XXVIII–LXXVII from the first Christmas (1833) after Arthur's death to the first anniversary of his death; Second Cycle LXXVIII–CIII from the second Christmas (1834) to the second anniversary of his death; Third Cycle CIV–CXXXI from Christmas (1837) to the end of the individual poems; and the Epilogue. This is the cyclical arrangement that Gatty[14] and Genung used as the basis of their analyses. The chronological evidences in the poem provided the framework for Tennyson's own division into nine sections: I–VIII, IX–XX, XXI–XXVII, XXVIII–XLIX, L–LVIII, LIX–LXXI, LXXII–XCVIII, XCIX–CIII, CIV–CXXXI.[15]

[10] Thomas Davidson, *Prolegomena to "In Memoriam"* (Boston, 1897).

[11] Charles F. G. Masterman, *Tennyson as a Religious Teacher* (London, 1900).

[12] Hoxie Neale Fairchild, *Religious Trends in English Poetry, 1830–1880* (New York, 1957), IV, 113–121.

[13] Jerome Hamilton Buckley, *Tennyson: The Growth of a Poet* (Cambridge, Mass., 1960).

[14] Alfred Gatty, *A Key to Lord Tennyson's "In Memoriam"* (London, 1885).

[15] George Benjamin Woods and Jerome Hamilton Buckley (eds.), *Poetry of the Victorian Period* (New York, 1955), p. 970 n.

The attempts at detailed coherent analysis of the interrelationships of the elegies have failed because they have tried either to prove a preconceived idea concerning the poet's religious faith or to establish a tight philosophical development of thought. One obvious approach to a modern elegy would be to discover if it bears any significant resemblance to the classical elegy. Imbedded within its informal and conversational manner, *In Memoriam* contains many of the classical elegiac conventions. The poem begins with the invocation to a higher power—"Strong Son of God"—and in poem XXXVII it seeks the aid of Melpomene, muse of lofty poetry. The voyage of Hallam's corpse might be considered a funeral procession with all nature mourning his death. In accordance with the traditions of the classical elegy, Tennyson moves from personal grief to a consideration of broad and lofty themes concerning the reality of God's purpose in history and the world, as well as his own destiny as a man and a poet. Poem XCV provides an apotheosis, and the Epilogue draws all to an epithalamic conclusion of mourning and death issuing in marriage, birth and new life.[16] The classical elegiac conventions are observed, but not in such a way as to provide either a framework for the whole or dividing lines within the work.

The best analysis can be made by imitating Tennyson's own method of composition and arrangement. The one continuous thread upon which all is arranged is the poet's thought of Arthur Hallam. This should be indicated first and primarily. Then the beads of various size and type may be placed upon the thread in the place Tennyson put them, not where the development of thought might make them logical or appropriate. Thus this study uses the nine main divisions Tennyson suggested in attempting to string the beads of his thought on the thread of his sorrow.

The Prologue, written last, is a summary and digest of the

[16] Arthur J. Carr, "Tennyson as a Modern Poet," *University of Toronto Quarterly*, XIX (July 1950), 361–382.

thought of the whole, rather than an introduction to it. The Son of God, Who is immortal love, is known to us only by means of faith, for we can neither see Him nor prove His existence. He made man, who thinks he is not to suffer extinction at death because of the justice of God. Our philosophies and sciences provide only fleeting glimpses of Him Who is more than they. We trust that our faith comes from God; may it grow! Let knowledge grow, too, but linked with reverence, so that the knowing mind and the faithful soul may be in harmony. The poet needs to be forgiven for his sense of his own worth, for merit is a word to use about human relationships, not about the divine-human encounter. He needs forgiveness for these wild and wandering cries of grief. He asks for God's wisdom by which to comfort his grief and understand his world.

Following Tennyson's own divisions of the elegy, the first section (poems I–VIII) is a mingling of love and grief. Spring may come, but not for Arthur. Sorrow teaches that nature is blind and careless. The poet feels it is almost sinful to try to express all the grief he feels even though poetic composition numbs his pain. So he leaves a poem, since his poems pleased the beloved when he was still alive.

Section two (IX–XX) traces the voyage of Arthur's remains. The poet's spirit flies to the corpse, and returning, asks, "Is this the end?" He wishes he could breathe life back into his friend, but, powerless to do so, the poet is left with "calm despair" and "wild unrest."

In the third section (XXI–XXVII) the poet examines the effect of his loss upon himself. Do these elegies prove that he is weak, an exhibitionist, antisocial, a seeker after refuge from life? No, he sings simply "because I must." Because love and sharing made the day's burden light, he will prove that time cannot canker love, for he knows it is better to have loved and lost than never to have loved.

Section four (XXVIII–XLIX) opens with the first Christmas after Arthur's death, celebrated "sadly," with a vain pretense of gaiety. Mary rejoiced single-heartedly in the resurrection of her brother Lazarus, without asking metaphysical questions about his days and nights spent in the tomb. Some with such a simple faith may depend upon the "forms" of conventional religion. Others who have achieved a "purer" faith without such forms must try to live as well as the former, for immortality is necessary to give man a conscience and life an aim. Man's love would be the lust of satyrs if there were no immortality. Urania rebukes the poet, reminding him that "faith has many a purer priest" and "abler voice." He should go down to Melpomene, an "earthly Muse" who mourns and darkens "sanctities with song." As a baby develops the isolation of personal identity, so Arthur may develop an immortal identity; yet he will never forget his five years of friendship with the poet, nor be merged into a general soul. The poet makes his first *apologia*: these poems are not systematic answers to doubt, but doubt made vassal to love.

In section five (L–LVIII) the tone changes to bitter questioning and violent doubts. The poet's faith burns low and he paints a picture of time as a maniac scattering dust, of life as a fury slinging flame, of men as flies. Philosophy, pushed beyond her rightful sphere, can become "procuress to the Lords of Hell." We must trust that good can arise out of evil, that each life is of value, and that all life has purpose. But the poet is no wiser than an "infant crying for the light" and he has "no language but a cry." Evolutionary theory suggests that nature is careful of the species but careless of the single life, and in despair the poet falls upon God's altar stairs, faintly trusting "the larger hope." Geology replies that nature is careless of species, too, cares for nothing, is red in tooth and claw, and veils all final answers from human minds. Urania now promises the poet that she will inspire "a nobler leave" of the dead.

Section six (LIX–LXXI) is an attempt to domesticate sorrow. The poet will live with sorrow as with a wife; he will love the deceased as a girl loves a man of higher social rank.

Let Arthur look upon the poet as upon a favorite horse or hound, or like a great man remembering a poor boyhood friend, for love is too precious to be lost, the friends are part each of the other. Dreaming, he has to struggle to visualize Arthur's face, yet dreams have the power to make the past present.

Section seven (LXXII–XCVIII) starts with the problem of unrealized potentiality and the deceased's fame. Although the world may not care how great Arthur might have become, there is a "tumult of acclaim" in Heaven. The poet's elegy will be forgotten in fifty years, but still he must "breathe my loss" and "utter love." The second Christmas is observed "calmly" with a "quiet sense of something lost." At the second New Year since his death, winter is like sorrow in the poet's blood. He pictures Arthur as husband to Emily Tennyson, as the father of children, as an old man dying along with the poet. He begs a newer friend, Edmund Lushington, who married Cecilia Tennyson in 1842, to understand that he "cannot transfer the whole I felt from him to you." Nature, "sweet after showers," dispels doubt and death and whispers, "Peace." Standing outside Arthur's old room at Trinity College, Cambridge, he remembers the debates of "The Apostles" and how eagerly they all listened to Arthur's superior mind and spirit. He recalls the times when Arthur came down from his law studies to visit Somersby, and the long talks and walks. The poet rejects spiritualism by which to communicate with the dead, but as Christ returned in the form of the Holy Ghost, may the poet's ghost feel the presence of Arthur's. But the communication he despaired of from spiritualism and hoped for from religion comes to him in a vision and apotheosis as he reads Arthur's letters on the lawn at Somersby. With him, he is carried up into the empyrean and catches a glimpse of the universe as it looks to the illustrious dead, before all is canceled by doubt and he is back on the lawn again. Was this doubt from the Devil? But Arthur won through to a higher faith by the path of honest doubt. The sight of a married couple makes him think of his own "spirit as a wife" and of how contentedly Arthur and he could have lived together like a devoted couple.

The eighth is a very brief section (XCIX–CIII) beginning with the second anniversary of Arthur's death and closing with a strange allegorical dream of reunion. On this second anniversary the poet recognizes his fellowship with all those who mourn. As he makes ready to leave Somersby for High Beech, Epping Forest, all the familiar scenery reminds him of Arthur. He realizes that the memory of his family will fade from those familiar hills and he mixes love of home and love of Arthur in one image of regret. The night before departure he dreamed a dream which made him content to face the morn. Probably based upon the parable of the Virgins and the Lamps,[17] he dreams that he lives in a hall with many maidens. A call comes for him to leave, and with them he takes a voyage, presumably the voyage of death. They increase in size and stateliness before they reach the sea and the ship, where they find him whom they loved, thrice life-sized. The poet and the dead are reunited, the maidens are permitted to enter the bridal feast and the ship sails away toward a crimson cloud.

The ninth section (CIV–CXXXI) begins with a third Christmas since the death of Arthur, "strangely" observed in a strange house. The wild bells of New Year's Eve are interpreted by the poet to ring out not only the old year but grief, social and economic inequality, poverty, sin, disease, war, and avarice. They are to ring in a nobler cause, a higher manhood, the "Christ that is to be." February 1, Arthur's birthday, is a "bitter" (cold) day in which they drink to his memory and sing the songs he loved. The poet resolves that he must not isolate himself from other lives, now that even death has for him a human face. He recalls the power of Arthur's conversation and how he rejoiced in his triumphs and felt a vague desire to imitate him. The poet is often tempted to prefer "narrower

[17] The Gospel According to Matthew, Chapter XXV.

perfectness" to "glorious insufficiencies," but Arthur had amplitude that never failed. He could have guided not only the poet's life, but also the nation and its parliament. Knowledge is great and must increase, but it has no power in the face of death. It, being earthly, must defer to wisdom, which is heavenly and of the soul. The world should grow like Arthur, not only in power and knowledge, but also in reverence and charity. Consider the work of time in forming the earth from flaming nebulae, in creating man and transmitting his acquired characteristics like the refining and tempering of steel. Man must flee the satyr, the faun, the sensual riot of the passions, and move upward, letting "the ape and tiger die." In a second *apologia*, the poet hopes his songs have not been wasted breath, that existence is not merely the magnetic theory of the brain. As Paul fought with beasts in the arena, so he has fought with death in these elegies. Science may prove evolution but it cannot make him think himself a "greater ape." As Hesper and Phosphor, the evening and the morning star, are two names for the one planet Venus, so the past and the present have become one in him. Having invoked Christ, Melpomene and Urania in previous sections, now he invokes Arthur to dwell in him and inspire his poetry. Geology may record the leveling of mountains and the drying up of seas, but he cannot believe that his farewell to Arthur is a final one, for feeling reveals deeper truths about God, the world, and human life than science or reason. In a third *apologia* he reminds the reader that even if his songs sometimes were bitter or contradictory, he never completely let go of hope, love, or truth. "Love is and was" his "lord and king," bringing messages from Arthur from afar and whispering in the night that "all is well." Social justice will triumph even in spite of the "fool-fury" of revolution, and Arthur will glimpse all these earthly happenings and smile, knowing "all is well." Love which met death unafraid is a greater comrade of the lesser faith in human progress, but now the poet sees that life, like art, is "toil cooperant to an end." The poet mixes Arthur and the universe in a pantheistic vision in which his friend becomes earth's animating spirit. He closes the elegies with a benediction addressed to the God Who gives men the will to endure, Who hears men's prayers, Who works in partnership with men. Men must trust the truths that cannot be proved, through faith that comes from self-control, until at last we are united with all we have loved.

In the Epithalamium, the poet begs Edmund Lushington not to request a poem celebrating his marriage to Cecilia Tennyson, although the event makes him happier than any since Arthur Hallam had first spoken to him of his love for Emily Tennyson, nine years before. The poet then describes the bride and the groom and the moment at noon when he gives his sister away. The wedding takes place above tombs, and memorial tablets are all about on the walls. Thus, by association, the "grave" of Arthur is bright with joy and promise. The wedding is over, the reception past, the married couple has departed. The poet asks the moon tenderly to touch the doors of their bridal chamber that there may be conceived in their embrace a soul "from out the vast" which will be a link between present humanity and the "crowning race" to come, a race of whom the friend he once knew and always loved was a "noble type," that friend who dwells with the God Who lives and loves and moves the whole creation toward "one far-off divine event."

The foregoing analysis establishes several points and corrects others. First, it is impossible to say that the poem is personal at the beginning and then becomes general, philosophical, scientific, and theological. It is apparent that the poet's personal relationship with Arthur Henry Hallam is omnipresent in his thought and in all of the elegies.[18] This was indeed, an exceptional friendship, as William Gladstone pointed out— "what can be a nobler tribute than this, that for seventeen years after his death, a poet, fast rising towards the lofty summits of his art, found that young fading image

[18] Buckley, *Tennyson*, p. 110.

the richest source of his inspiration, and of thoughts that gave him buoyancy for a flight such as he had not hitherto attained?" [19]

Second, the passages which deal with the existence of God, His plan and purpose in the world, the work of Christ, and the certainty of immortality reveal that doubt is as strong as hope; certainty is never expressed, faith is always cautious and tentative. This dubiety, far from being a liability, endeared the verses to the critical thinkers of his generation who did not assume that the poem proved immortality. "The best and bravest of my contemporaries," said James Anthony Froude, "determined to have done with insincerity, to find ground under their feet, to let the uncertain remain uncertain, but to learn how much and what we could honestly regard as true, and to believe that and live by it. Tennyson became the voice of this feeling in poetry, Carlyle in what was called prose. . . . Tennyson's Poems, the group of Poems which closed with *In Memoriam*, became to many of us what *The Christian Year* was to orthodox Churchmen. We read them, and they became part of our minds, the expression, in exquisite language of the feelings which were working in ourselves." [20] The classical study of Tennyson as a religious thinker, and still by far the best, was published by Charles F. G. Masterman in 1900. In strict but masterly fashion he sums up the characteristics of Tennyson's faith:

All his discussion and speculation concerning the nature of God, Self, or Immortality [in *In Memoriam*] ultimately terminated in this position:—There are indications pointing to the existence of an all-perfect God, to the reality of the Self, to the Immortality of each individual personality. And then again there are facts of experience which seem directly to deny these possibilities. The only possibility is *faith* that these represent

[19] William Ewart Gladstone, "Review of *In Memoriam*," *Gleanings of Past Years* (New York, 1886), II, 136–137.

[20] James Anthony Froude, *Thomas Carlyle: A History of His Life in London* (New York, 1910), p. 248.

realities and not illusions; all other theories leave life meaningless, and effort vain. We must cling to the hope that some day
we shall be answered and vindicated in our belief.

In the narrower sense he was not a religious poet; in the
wider sense he was not a teacher of religion . . . personal
devotion to Christ, personal experience of sin, direct consciousness of the presence of God, these do not in any way
furnish the *motifs* of his poems. On the other hand, he did not
maintain any unwavering attitude of triumph and optimistic
conviction, which would have enabled him to teach a new
creed, or proclaim a new religion. He was too uncertain of
himself; his faith often grew dim; he was striving, for the most
part, in the dark, with only at intervals uncertain gleams of
light . . . often the horizon appeared to him to be darkening,
and his religion rather the last refuge of despair, than the
joyful assertion of firm belief. Right on until the end, sadness
and hope, doubt and faith alternately reveal themselves in
his writings. [21]

A more recent critic of Tennyson as religious thinker, Hoxie
Neale Fairchild, agrees essentially with Masterman's analysis.
He, too, finds Tennyson an "emotional pragmatist" [22] rather
than a Christian mystic. But in his agreement, he reminds us
of two other facets of the thought of *In Memoriam* that should
be noted: the primacy of feeling and the solution of love.
Tennyson's crucial reply to the freezing queries of doubt, "I
have felt" (CXXIV), can be related to Arthur Hallam's
prose statement: "we have not the slightest reason for supposing that the operations of our thoughts approach nearer to the
modes of Divine Knowledge, than the affections of our hearts
to that Love, which God is." [23] The "solution of love" is borne
out in the thought and works of other contemporaries, as well.
Consider Robert Browning's oft-quoted line from "An
Epistle": "So, the All-Great, were the All-loving too" (line
305), and the great climax of the eighteenth section of "Saul":

---

[21] Masterman, *Tennyson as a Religious Teacher*, pp. 46, 237.

[22] Fairchild, *Religious Trends in English Poetry*, IV, 119.

[23] Motter, *Arthur Hallam*, p. 212.

> O Saul, it shall be
> A Face like my face that receives thee; a Man like to me,
> Thou shalt love and be loved by, forever; a Hand like this
>   hand
> Shall throw open the gates of new life to thee! See the
>   Christ stand! [lines 309–312]

As a matter of fact this second reference is startlingly like Tennyson in another way. God's face will be like David's face, He will be a man like David, and have a hand like his, and the gates open and there the Christ stands (in defiance of Biblical chronology). Tennyson's treatment of Christ is very similar. Of His redemptive work, not a word; but much as a type of the higher, nobler manhood, of which also Arthur Hallam is a type, so much so that Arthur and the Christ figure merge to become not only the second Person of the Trinity, but in the pantheistic passage (CXXX) the third Person, as well.

Tennyson's argument for the solution of love is similar to William Makepeace Thackeray's in *The Newcomes*: "if love lives through all life; and survives through all sorrow; and remains steadfast with us through all changes; and in all darkness of spirit burns brightly; and, if we die, deplores us forever, and loves still equally; and exists with the very last gasp and throb of the faithful bosom—whence it passes with the pure soul, beyond death; surely it shall be immortal!" [24] Nor was it a new discovery for Tennyson at the time of the great elegy. In 1830 he wrote the lines "On Cambridge University," tactfully suppressed all the rest of his career, closing, "you that do profess to teach / And teach us nothing, feeding not the heart." Also in 1830, in the poem "Love and Death," which might almost have served for a preliminary study of several poems (XLIII, CXXVI, Epilogue) of *In Memoriam*, Love is expelled from Paradise by Death. Love leaves, weeping, but replies that death is only the shadow of

---

[24] *The Works of William Makepeace Thackeray* (London, 1907), VI: *The Newcomes*, chapter 45, 489.

life, and when life ends love "shall reign for ever over all." Along with the apotheosis of Section XCV, the passages "'I have felt'" (CXXIV) and "Love is and was my lord and king" (CXXVI) are the great climactic moments of the poem.

But the "solutions" of faith and of love are never real solutions for Tennyson. Clutched in desperation, they do not quite bear the full weight of his anguish for certainty. He turns to faith only in the default of reason, and to the continuity of love only because he cannot be sure of the continuity of life through immortality. And he must believe in immortality both for Hallam's sake and for the sake of morality, for the ethical sanction arises not from the integral value of right as right, but from the belief that there is judgment and continued life beyond.

Before we move on to an examination of the relationship of science to Tennyson's religious faith and faith in progress, it might be well to establish Tennyson's philosophical and religious position as part of a continuing position in traditional philosophy and English letters. Ever since Pyrrho of Elis, 365–275 B.C., there has been a well-defined position of literary-philosophical skepticism to any and all metaphysical assertions.[25] Against every proposition, the wise man will balance its contrary and consequently, by showing the futility of both, will arrive at the happy state of imperturbability ($\dot{a}\tau a\rho\dot{a}\xi\iota a$). But since no moral standard can be established absolutely by reason, the wise man will conform to the laws and conventions he finds generally accepted by other men.

In the great elegy, pondered for seventeen years, there are numerous passages which reflect Tennyson's uncertainty and his unwillingness to accept or make dogmatic philosophic assertions. Poem LIV confesses—"Behold, we know not anything," and in an ultimate reduction of the power of reason, says of the self:

[25] L. I. Bredvold, *The Intellectual Milieu of John Dryden* (Ann Arbor, 1934), pp. 17 ff.

So runs my dream, but what am I?
An infant crying in the night;
An infant crying for the light,
And with no language but a cry.

But doubt of the power of the human mind to know anything with certainty, while present in the poem, never becomes
the single tone of the poem. Stemming from Augustine and
presented most forcefully to the modern world through the
essays of Montaigne, a special form of limited Pyrrhonism can
be distinguished from that general skepticism which is doubtful
about any kind of ontological assertion. These two thinkers
accept skepticism in only one area of epistemology, the possibility of knowledge of the nonmaterial world achieved through
the senses. For them, reason was definitely limited to the
scope of knowledge of material being delivered through the
senses. But faith ("Fide-ism") can know in ways impossible
to the reason. A very fine literary example of Fideism is found
in Sir Thomas Browne's *Religio Medici*: "thus I teach my
haggard and unreclaimed reason to stoop to the lure of Faith.
. . . And this I think is no vulgar part of Faith, to believe a
thing not only above, but contrary to Reason, and against the
Arguments of our proper Senses." And even more vigorously:
"Methinks there be no impossibilities enough in Religion for
an active faith. . . . I love to lose myself in a mystery, to
pursue my Reason to an *O altitudo*!" A poetic example of
Fideism is found in the opening lines of Dryden's *Religio Laici*,
written in 1682, about fifty years after the similarly named
work by Browne:

Dim as the borrow'd beams of Moon and Stars
To lonely, weary, wand'ring Travellers
Is Reason to the Soul: And as on high
Those rowling Fires discover but the Sky
Not light us here; So Reason's glimmering Ray
Was lent, not to assure our doubtfull way,
But guide us upward to a better Day.

And as those nightly Tapers disappear
When Day's bright Lord ascends our Hemisphere;
So pale grows Reason at Religion's sight;
So dyes, and so dissolves in Supernatural Light.
[lines 1–11]

There are some notable expressions of Fideism in *In Memoriam*, particularly in the Prologue, the last part of the poem to be composed and thus significant as giving the central and integrating viewpoint of the whole:

Strong Son of God, immortal Love
    Whom we that have not seen thy face,
    By faith, and faith alone, embrace,
Believing where we cannot prove. . . .

We have but faith; we cannot know,
    For knowledge is of things we see;
    And yet we trust it comes from thee,
A beam in darkness; let it grow.
[lines 1–4, 21–24]

A fragmentation of poem CXIV to pick out the key words shows the contrast between the knowledge of mind and sense and the wisdom of revelation and faith: "Knowledge. . . . Let her know her place; / She is the second, not the first . . . earthly of the mind. . . . Wisdom heavenly of the soul." Anna Krause recognized this characteristic of Fideism in Tennyson and related it to the writings of the Spanish poet-mystic Unamuno: "Philosophical concepts common to both poets are analyzed here—the ultimate nature of reality, the problem of knowledge with its distinction between the knowing mind and the believing soul (knowledge being of things we 'see,' sense perception, rational proof), faith transcending the veil of sense and reason to intuit a personal God." [26]

The relevance of this literary-philosophic excursion becomes clear the moment we ask, "Was Tennyson a thorough-going

[26] Anna Krause, "Unamuno and Tennyson," *Comparative Literature*, VIII (1956), 130.

Pyrrhonist or Fideist?" The only possible answer is, "Neither." A real skeptic would be willing to say, finally and with some peace of mind, that we simply cannot know and must go on our way without knowing. Tennyson says we cannot know, but we must know if we are to go on our way at all. The Fideist would never say, "We have *but* faith," for faith is not something to fall back on in desperation when reason fails. It is a higher instrument to use joyfully and confidently to lead us to warm and firm affirmations of spiritual existence which can be arrived at through no lesser means. Whereas the best Tennyson can do is to fall back on verbs like "trust," "hope," "seems." Philosophically, just as every other way, the poet would affirm, but cannot; would withdraw, but dare not. The tension remains. Jesus was willing to perform a miracle for a man who cried, "Lord, I believe; help thou mine unbelief." [27] The literary critic needs to exercise a similar "existentialism" and admit that contrasting qualities may be present in the same mind at the same or alternating moments, and that to ignore either is to miss the real personal issue for the poet.

The "Supposed Confessions of a Second-Rate Sensitive Mind," written before Tennyson was twenty-one, published in 1830 and suppressed for fifty years thereafter, begins with the isolation of the artist but quickly moves into the tension of doubt and faith. The subject of the poem longs to be numbered with those for whom Christ died, to be a "Christian with happy countenance," to share "the common faith" and the "common scorn of death," to respond to his mother's prayers that he be reconciled to her God. He even argues sophistically with himself:

> Why not believe then? Why not yet
> Anchor thy frailty there, where man
> Hath moor'd and rested? [lines 123–125]

He recognizes his past pride, "the sin of devils," but now feels that pride has left, leaving him "void, dark, formless, utterly

[27] The Gospel According to Mark, IX, 24.

destroyed." He speaks of belief by an act of coercive will, but immediately asserts, "It is man's privilege to doubt," just as twenty years later, when his apotheosis with Arthur's spirit was canceled by doubt (*In Memoriam*, XCV) he asked if doubt was from the devil, but then balanced that question by recalling that Arthur had won through to faith by the hard road of honest doubt. In the "Supposed Confessions" there follow two unforgettably poignant and powerful pictures of death, which is obviously the crux of his fear:

> on his light there falls
> A shadow; and his native slope,
> Where he was wont to leap and climb,
> Floats from his sick and filmed eyes,
> And something in the darkness draws
> His forehead earthward, and he dies
>
> and the busy fret
> Of that sharp-headed worm begins
> In the gross blackness underneath.
>
> [lines 163–168, 185–187]

Here is a true "metaphysical shudder," not now in the seventeenth century, but the nineteenth. "Two questions: Who am I, Why do I exist? and the panic fear of their remaining unanswered—doubt is much too intellectual and tame a term for such a vertigo of anxiety—seem to have obsessed him all his life." [28] Fairchild also reminds us, as the "Supposed Confessions" does, that we ought not to infer from "Vastness," "In the Valley of Cauteretz," or even from *In Memoriam*, that Tennyson's craving for immortality was solely the consequence of his love for Arthur Hallam. "Even if his friend had never existed, the master-passion would have been no less intense. . . . We do not know why his desire for immortality was so passionate. Perhaps it was his strongest belief because it was also his deepest dread." [29]

[28] W. H. Auden (ed.), *A Selection from the Poems of Alfred, Lord Tennyson* (Garden City, 1944), xvi.

[29] Fairchild, *Religious Trends in English Poetry*, p. 114.

The "Supposed Confessions" closes with the famous lines which illustrate so well the contention that when he was young and when he was old the poet was unable to accept either of any two alternatives—and he knew it.

> O weary life! O weary death!
> O spirit and heart made desolate!
> O damned vacillating state!
>
> [lines 188–190]

"The Ancient Sage," published fifty-five years later, in 1885, and shot through with the by then familiar device of interwoven songs, has a line which is richly humorous advice, because it is the one bit of counsel the poet was incapable of accepting—"Cleave ever to the sunnier side of doubt. . . ." This curious counsel, neither courageous skepticism nor vigorous conviction, was almost parodied by G. M. Young in his article "The Age of Tennyson"—"a philosophy of Somehow, wavering between a hopeful doubt and a doubtful hope." [30] Tennyson himself never chose the sunny side of doubt, because seeing both sun and shadow, he had to record and feel both. If the balance is drawn, Nicolson is probably right in saying that he is "more convincing in doubt than in faith." [31]

> Thou canst not prove the Nameless, O my son,
> Nor canst thou prove the world thou movest in,
> Thou canst not prove that thou art body alone,
> Nor canst thou prove that thou art spirit alone,
> Nor canst thou prove that thou art both in one.
> Thou canst not prove thou art immortal, no,
> Nor yet that thou art mortal—nay, my son,
> Thou canst not prove that I, who speak with thee,
> Am not thyself in converse with thyself,
> For nothing worthy proving can be proven,
> Nor yet disproven.
>
> ["The Ancient Sage," lines 57–67]

[30] G. M. Young, "The Age of Tennyson," in John Killham (ed.), *Critical Essays on the Poetry of Tennyson* (London, 1960), p. 39.
[31] Nicolson, *Tennyson*, p. 126.

This is a litany of doubt with a wistful postcript of hope. Everything is without intellectual certainty: religion and agnosticism, materialism and spiritualism, idealism and interactionism, immortality and mortality, both the Cartesian *Cogito ergo sum* and Humian solipsism. The end is neither skepticism nor certainty; it is a longing, unsure faith in something which can never be known as the poet wishes to know it.

Whatever our view of Tennyson as an original thinker, he kept well abreast of the new movements in thought during his century, particularly as his poetry reflects the impact of the sciences on the mind of his generation. Even before he became England's "official poet" as Laureate, he seems to have felt challenged to illustrate in his own works what Wordsworth had prophesied in the Preface to his *Lyrical Ballads*: "If the labours of Men of science should ever create any material revolution, direct or indirect, in our condition, and in the impressions which we habitually receive, the Poet will sleep then no more than at present; he will be ready to follow the steps of the Man of science, not only in those general indirect effects, but he will be at his side carrying sensation into the midst of the objects of the science itself." [32] An examination of Tennyson's scientific thought should consider his poems chronologically, since each decade of the nineteenth century brought new and startling scientific discoveries for its thinkers to receive and assimilate.

The "still small voice" of despair in "The Two Voices" (1833) confronted the Biblical cosmogony of the poet:

> "When first the world began
> Young Nature thro' five cycles ran,
> And in the sixth she moulded man."
>
> [lines 16–18]

[32] William Wordsworth, "Of the Principles of Poetry and His *Lyrical Ballads*" (1798–1802), in Alexander B. Grosart (ed.), *The Prose Works of William Wordsworth* (London, 1876), p. 91.

with modern astronomy and its meaningless immensity of space: "the world is wide . . . a boundless universe . . . yonder hundred million spheres." *"L'Envoi"* (1842) of "The Day-Dream" (1830) trumpets that uncertain sound which might be celebration or dismay. The poet speaks of the delights of falling asleep with all one's friends to wake each hundred years "on science grown to more, / On secrets of the brain, the stars, / As wild as aught of fairy lore." Read one way, the poet seems to take pleasure in the growth of scientific knowledge, which is as marvelous as magic. Read the other way, the poet is glad to sleep through the difficult years of science's struggle with religion and wake at last to find all a *fait accompli*. We have already noted the poet's tension between the desire to retreat and the willingness to participate. In "Locksley Hall" (1842) he again likens the marvels of science to fairy lore—"the fairy tales of science" (line 12)—and adds to its present marvels a prophecy of what science will produce in the future, and again the picture is ambiguous. There will be airships filling the heavens with commerce, "argosies of magic sails, / Pilots of the purple twilight, dropping down with costly bales." But the heavens will also be filled with "shouting" and will rain "a ghastly dew" as the airships of the nations grapple "in the central blue" (lines 121–124). As for the scientific wonders of "the steamship . . . the railway . . . the thoughts that shake mankind" (lines 166 ff.), the young hunter thinks there would be more pleasure in summer islands where passions are no longer cramped and life has scope and men have space to breathe. He finally votes to remain in England with the "march of mind," but he nowhere suggests that this is a pleasanter or more desirable destiny.

In the 1833 edition of "The Palace of Art," the passage "From change to change four times within the womb / The brain is moulded" probably refers to Cuvier's theory of the fetal development of the brain through the four stages of fish, reptile, bird and human, and "More complex is more perfect, owning more / Discourse, more widely wise" relates to the anthropological supposition that the more complex the organism, the more recently it fits into the geological age schedule.

John Killham has a splendid section, in his recent book, on the scientific allusions to be found in Tennyson's *The Princess*.[33] The curriculum of Princess Ida's University for Women includes electricity and chemistry, and the Princess had long made mathematics and astronomy her special interest. We are told that she passed whole nights with Psyche in a tower, talking about "sine and arc, spheroid, azimuth and right ascension." The male invaders in their female garb are taken on an odd combination picnic-geological expedition where shale and hornblende, rag and trap and tuff are discussed learnedly by their hostesses. E. A. Mooney has pointed out the bearing of the Herschel-Laplace nebular hypothesis on the lines "was once a fluid haze of light, / Till toward the centre set the starry tides, / And eddied into suns, that wheeling cast / The planets." [34] When the fossilized bones of a prehistoric mammoth are exposed to the picnic party by the cutting back of a waterfall, the princess "gazed awhile and said, 'As these rude bones to us, are we to her / That will be.'" (Lyell discussed the significance of the cutting back of Niagara and the entombment of a mastodon in his *Travels in North America*.[35] The Prince's great final peroration at the close of Part VII gives one evidence of Tennyson's early grasp of the sociological relevance of many of the staggering hypotheses of biology: "The woman's cause is man's; they rise or sink / Together. . . . If she be small, slight-natured, miserable, / How shall men grow?" But an even more striking illustration is found in Tennyson's use of Lamarck's theory of Functional Reaction. According to this theory, which was soon discarded, the production of a new organ in an animal results from a new need

[33] John Killham, *Tennyson and "The Princess": Reflections of an Age* (London, 1958), pp. 230 ff.

[34] E. A. Mooney, "A Note on Astronomy in Tennyson's *The Princess*," *MLN*, LXIV (1949), 98.

[35] Charles Lyell, *Travels in North America* (London, 1845), pp. 27–53.

which continues to be felt and then after its development is repeated in all the offspring of that animal. This is usually referred to as the theory of the inheritance of acquired characteristics. It was for the sake of this theory that George Bernard Shaw always described himself as an anti-Darwinian Lamarckian, because only through such inheritance was there hope for human progress. Tennyson refers to the theory in the same seventh section of *The Princess* by using the technical word "type," which meant to him and contemporary scientists, "to place a characteristic in the line of inheritance": "'Dear, but let us type them now / In our own lives.'" By uniting the finest human qualities, a "crowning race of humankind" will be produced and "the statelier Eden" brought back to earth. The full significance of this "typology" does not come completely to view until we examine the scientific allusions in *In Memoriam*.

In the third poem of *In Memoriam*, 1850, Sorrow whispers to the poet that the stars move "blindly," that the sun is "dying," that all Nature is "empty" of purpose and of God. The poet is sufficiently aware of the scientific theories of planetary attraction, the heat-loss of the solar system, and a completely naturalistic philosophy to reject them. In poem XXXV he hears the sound of rushing streams and realizes that through erosion they are carrying mountains down to the sea and heaping up "the dust of continents to be." Poems LV and LVI are especially related to biology and geology. Are God and Nature "at strife," when Nature scatters fifty seeds and brings only one to flower and fruit? She seems to care nothing for the individual and everything for the species, and perhaps this is true also of her dealing with men. The next poem conveys an even darker truth: She is careless of species, as the fossils of forgotten types in every cliff give abundant evidence. God and Nature are at strife, and when our faith teaches us that the law of life is love, Nature shrieks defiantly that the spirit is only the breath and that man himself shall someday be superseded and his remains will be blown about the desert or "seal'd within the iron hills."

Nature is "red in tooth and claw" and men might just as well live as the predatory monsters lived in prehistoric times. Poem CXIV contains the celebrated distinction between knowledge, which is "earthly of the mind," or in other words, dependent upon the data of the senses, and Wisdom, which is "heavenly of the soul" and grows by intuition and faith out of men's need to understand. Knowledge, which is unable to give hope to one who has lost a friend, must take second place to Wisdom, which gives hope even in bereavement. Poem CXVII is probably the most concentratedly scientific in the entire elegy; containing references to the Herschel-Laplace Nebular Hypothesis—"the solid earth. . . . In tracts of fluent heat began . . . seeming-random forms, / The seeming prey of cyclic storms"; a pre-Darwinian theory of evolution—men arising from a "branch'd" family tree; Lamarckian inheritance of acquired characteristics—"the herald of a higher race. . . . If so he type this work of time"; moral evolution which accompanies physical evolution—"fly / The reeling Faun, the sensual feast; / Move upward"; and a pre-Freudian depth psychology— "working out the beast, / And let the ape and tiger die." Poem CXX, although not published until 1850, was actually written before and in some items anticipates Robert Chambers' *Vestiges of the Natural History of Creation*, published in 1844. Both point out that the activities of the brain seem to be of an electrical nature, but Tennyson insists that even if scientists base theories on "cunning casts in clay" and sum up the brain as magnetism, and teach youth that they are "greater apes," he was "born to other things." There is a family relationship of thought between poem CXXIII and Darwin's famous passage in *The Voyage of the Beagle* when the naturalist stands on the crest of the Cordilleras. In Tennyson's words:

> There rolls the deep where grew the tree.
>   O earth, what changes hast thou seen!
>   There where the long street roars hath been
> The stillness of the central sea.

The hills are shadows, and they flow
  From form to form, and nothing stands;
  They melt like mist, the solid lands,
Like clouds they shape themselves and go.

while Darwin says:

We spent the day on the summit, and I never enjoyed one more thoroughly. Chile, bounded by the Andes and the Pacific, was seen as in a map. The pleasure from the scenery, in itself beautiful, was heightened by the many reflections which arose from the mere view of the Campana range with its lesser parallel ones, and of the broad valley of Quillota directly intersecting them. Who can avoid wondering at the force which has upheaved these mountains, and even more so at the countless ages which it must have required to have broken through, removed, and levelled whole masses of them? It is well in this case to call to mind the vast shingle and sedimentary beds of Patagonia, which, if heaped on the Cordillera, would increase its height by so many thousand feet. When in that country, I wondered how any mountain-chain could have supplied such masses, and not have been utterly obliterated. We must not now reverse the wonder, and doubt whether allpowerful time can grind down mountains—even the gigantic Cordillera—into gravel and mud.[36]

Poem CXXIV, one of the great climactic poems of the elegy, claims the priority of feeling over the doubt which comes from "freezing reason" "when faith had fallen asleep." The affirmation is the product of two forces: the horrible thought of a "Godless deep," and the recollection of the power of human love. Tennyson believes because he dare not doubt, he stands up "like a man in wrath" because the "warmth" of feeling has melted "freezing reason's colder part."

Earlier it was noted that the full significance of the "typology" of *The Princess* must wait upon an examination of the scientific allusions in *In Memoriam*. In the Epilogue of the latter poem we find the next to final quatrain:

[36] Charles Darwin, *The Voyage of the Beagle* (New York, 1909), p. 274.

> Whereof the man that with me trod
> This planet was a noble type
> Appearing ere the times were ripe,
> That friend of mine who lives in God.

In the former poem the prince and the princess were to "type" their superior characteristics through marriage and thus make their personal contribution to human evolutionary progress. But in the latter poem, Arthur, as the "type" of the noble race to come, is the closest we come to a true synthesis of the tension between the knowledge of science and the wisdom of faith. Four factors are involved: first, the general belief of the time that the movement of evolutionary progress from the simpler one-celled organism to the complexity of man represented an upward movement; second, that the Victorians lived in a transitional age in which everything was improving; third, that Hallam was that near-divinity, a biological "sport" which heralds a higher race of men; fourth, the Christian optimism that man is but "a little lower than the angels" somehow seeming to imply that he is progressing upward toward the angels, as Tennyson described elsewhere by the engravings on the walls of Camelot in the *Idylls of the King* representing men progressing from beasts to angels. Now, in a remarkable way Arthur Hallam almost becomes for Tennyson the reconciling factor of all these separate movements: he is a very good product of physical evolutionary process, he foreshadows a higher race to come, he is a representative type of the "Christ that is to be." From Tennyson's grief over the death of Hallam, his problem of making the ideal Arthur effective in an unideal world, and his deep-rooted conviction of the importance of marriage in which we participate in the cosmic purpose, there emerged a hierarchy of types, each higher than the preceding, but higher because of the achievements of the former lower level. Just as this hierarchy emerged from varied preoccupations of the poet, so it fused disparate and usually alien philosophies. Biologically this is evolution. Contemporaneously it was the Victorian ideal of progress.

Spiritually it preserved the Christian doctrine of the infinite value of the individual and the Protestant emphasis upon the sovereignty of the individual believer. The combination made evolution, the spirit of the age, and the coming of the Kingdom of God kinsmen and fellow travelers. "There is and has long been a growing disposition to think out old truth in new terms, to re-interpret, as it were by methods of spiritual science, the deathless ideas of God and revelation, and to discern, not only by the deliverances of logic but by the fine tactile instinct of the heart, wherein they are true to God and true to human nature." [37] All this represents a very high moment for Tennyson, the very closest he ever comes to a real synthesis of the theses and antitheses of life, as he almost combines the dearest friendship of his youth, evolutionary theory, and religious faith.

Hallam Tennyson's *Memoir* gives a splendid illustration of what the scientific orientation of the elegy meant to a contemporary philosopher and fellow member of the Metaphysical Society, Professor Henry Sidgwick:

What *In Memoriam* did for us, for me at least . . . was to impress on us the ineffaceable and ineradicable conviction that *humanity* will not and cannot acquiesce in a godless world. . . . The force with which it impressed this conviction was not due to the *mere intensity* of its expression of the feelings which Atheism outrages and Agnosticism ignores; but rather to its expression of them along with a reverent docility to the lessons of science which also belongs to the essence of the thought of our age. . . . Wordsworth's attitude towards Nature . . . left Science unregarded . . . known by simple observation and interpreted by religious and sympathetic intuition. But for your father the physical science: the scientific view of it dominates his thoughts about it; and his general acceptance of this view is real and sincere, even when he utters the intensest feeling of its inadequacy to satisfy our deepest needs. . . . Faith, in the introduction, is too triumphant. I

[37] James Martineau, *Essays Philosophical and Theological* (New York, 1875), I, 331.

think this is inevitable, because so far as the thought-debate presented by the poem is summed up, it must be summed up on the side of Faith. Faith must give the last word; but the last word is not the whole utterance and doubt must alternate in the moral world in which we at present live, somewhat as night and day alternate in the physical world. The revealing visions come and go; when they come we *feel* that we *know*; but in the intervals we must pass through states in which all is dark, and in which we can only struggle to hold the conviction that

> Power is with us in the night
> Which makes the darkness and the light
> And dwells not in the light alone.[38]

Professor Sidgwick's final statement exactly corresponds to the thought of this paper. Philosophically, Tennyson is neither a Pyrrhonist nor a Fideist. Scientifically, he is enough a child of the age to be "reverently docile" to the lessons of science and sensitive to currents of scientific thought as yet unpublished and unproved. Theologically, he believes in the existence of God, the working out of His purpose in the world, and personal immortality, not because he is intellectually convinced of their intrinsic truth and reality, but because he feels that otherwise life would be simply unbearable.

What the philosophies, all the sciences, poesy, varying voices
    of prayer,
All that is noblest, all that is basest, all that is filthy with
    all that is fair?

What is it all, if we all of us end but in being our own
    corpse-coffins at last?
Swallow'd in Vastness, lost in Silence, drown'd in the deeps
    of a meaningless Past?

What but a murmur of gnats in the gloom, or a moment's
    anger of bees in their hive?—

.　　.　　.　　.　　.　　.　　.　　.　　.　　.　　.

[38] Tennyson (Hallam), *Memoir*, II, 67 ff.

Peace, let it be! for I loved him, and love him for ever:
   the dead are not dead but alive.
        ["Vastness" (1885), XVI, XVII, XVIII]

The poet who never lost his interest in the contemporary
discoveries of science never lost his dread of what its philosophy
would mean to art, traditional beliefs, and the ethical sub-
structure of society. Whether the schoolboy was writing about
the spirit of Fable and his flight from Timbuctoo:

> O city! oh latest throne! where I was raised
> To be a mystery of loveliness
> Unto all eyes, the time is well-nigh come
> When I must render up this glorious home
> To keen Discovery.
>   ["Timbuctoo" (1829), lines 237–241]

or whether the octogenarian bard was writing about Parnassus
and the effect of science upon poetry and the poet's fame:

What be those two shapes high over the sacred fountain,
Taller than all the Muses, and huger than all the mountain?

.   .   .   .

Poet, that evergreen laurel is blasted by more than lightning!

.   .   .   .

These are Astronomy and Geology, terrible Muses!
      ["Parnassus" (1889), II, lines 1–2, 4, 8]

he recognizes the importance of science and the inevitability of
its advance, but at the same time he deplores its effect upon the
cultural treasures of the past, the world of the poet's imagination, the practice of art, and the validity of faith.

The poet's attitudes toward the Sovereignty and Providence
of God, personal immortality, and the new science have been
the chief foci of this chapter. He wants to believe in a God
Whose purposes are regnant in the universe, but if that universe

is dying and everywhere seems empty of the presence of God, he can only affirm, without evidence or conviction, that "the whole creation moves . . . To . . . one far-off divine event." He wants to believe that God not only rules but also loves his creatures, yet on every side he sees the carelessness of Nature— in wasted seed, torrents of babies, fossil-remains of extinct species, and the extinction of his own friend, Arthur. So because Tennyson's love has outlasted Hallam's life, he posits love as the nature of God and his own "lord and king." He wants desperately to believe that Arthur still lives and he is encouraged by the resurrection of Lazarus and an experience of mystical union with his departed friend. But the Biblical tale was meant for the simple faith of Mary and the mystical union was can- celed by doubt. So he can only affirm that there must be immortality because without it Arthur would be dead forever and the moral system would collapse if men knew they had but one brief life. He once believed and he wants to continue to believe that the advance of scientific knowledge contributes to the progress of the race. But when he sees what science has done to the lore of the past, the world of imagination, the doctrines of religion and the practice of the arts, he can only say that scientific reason must change the face of the world and revolu- tionize the lives of men; but only faith, unprovable and almost unidentifiable, can outlast death, comfort sorrow and restore meaning to the fading values of humanism.

As Sidgwick said, "Faith . . . and doubt must alternate in the moral world in which we at present live, somewhat as night and day alternate in the physical world. The revealing visions come and go; when they come we *feel* that we *know*: but in the intervals we must pass through states in which all is dark, and in which we can only struggle to hold the con- viction. . . ."

Or as Masterman wrote, "There are indications pointing to the existence of an all-perfect God, to the reality of the Self, to the Immortality of each individual personality. And then again there are facts of experience which seem directly to deny these possibilities. The only possibility is *faith* that these represent realities and not illusions. . . . We must cling to the hope that some day we shall be . . . vindicated in our belief . . . his faith often grew dim; he was striving, for the most part, in the dark, with only at intervals uncertain gleams of light. . . . Right on until the end, sadness and hope, doubt and faith alternately reveal themselves in his writings."

Tennyson himself described a mystical union which was broken, and an empyrean which was exchanged for "the doubtful dusk," the dark knolls and the "white kine" of this earth. As the dawn mixed the "dim lights" of East and West to illumine a dubious world of life and death, he could only hope it would someday "broaden into boundless day."

IV

Past versus Present

> What charm in words, a charm no words could give?
> O dying words, can Music make you live
> Far—far—away?

Tennyson need not have suggested that his little poem, "Far—Far—Away," 1889, be set to music. The "mystic pain and joy" of "those three words" which haunted him when he was a boy, haunted him always, and still haunt the reader, quite without the assistance of a musical score. His friend James Spedding remarked in 1835 that Tennyson was "a man always discontented with the Present till it has become the Past, and then he yearns toward it and worships it, and not only worships it, but is discontented because it is past." [1]

Spedding's comment succinctly states the contradictoriness and ambiguity of the poet's love of the past. In the present, he longs for the past; when the present has become the past he yearns for its return and magnifies it quite beyond the meanings it originally held; but when he finds that his interest lies buried in the past, he is conscience-stricken and must either return from it or fill it full of present meanings. His "worship" of the past is expressed in his power to take a legend or a myth and recreate it in language that sparkles and undulates with waves of presently felt emotion. His "discontent with the past" creates enrichment of meaning and value when the reader becomes aware that not only is he dealing with Ulysses or Demeter or Tiresias but also with Tennyson and the nineteenth

---

[1] Frances M. Brookfield, *The Cambridge "Apostles"* (New York, 1907), p. 268.

century and the ambivalence of the human spirit that made it seem perfectly appropriate to stage a tournament which was "*plus féodale que le moyen âge*" at the castle of the Earl of Eglinton and Winton, in the midst of a world of railroad trains, the rise of the commercial classes, and the first stirrings of the British labor movement.[2] Everywhere in Victorian England we see the lag of a feudal society and the thrust of a mercantile materialism, whether it is in the mingling of the two nations of mechanics and Cambridge students in the introduction to *The Princess*, in John Ruskin's defense of the use of Gothic architecture for a bank in a textile city, or in Walter Pater's praise of eclecticism: "Of such eclecticism we have a justifying example in one of the first poets of our time. How illustrative of monosyllabic effect, of sonorous Latin, of the phraseology of science, of metaphysic, of colloquialism even, are the writings of Tennyson; yet with what fine, fastidious scholarship throughout!"[3] Tennyson's recessive tendency, constantly corrected, makes him temperamentally as well as contemporaneously liable to mirror the conflict.[4]

Arthur J. Carr noted Tennyson's tendency to use myth and legend in a way that produced "a hard and brilliant surface of traditional substance under which the private sensibility moved as if through water."[5] As William Butler Yeats discovered half a century later, in 1927, Byzantium[6] is the place for the poet, a city of archetypal myth, where he may speak his mind but protect his heart by the "artifice of eternity."[7] Tennyson found in the past his self-protective Byzantium, where he was

[2] "The Eglinton Tournament," *Record*, III, 36; *Examiner*, XXX (July 14, 1839), 441; (Sept. 1), 555; (Sept. 8), 552.

[3] Walter Pater, "Style," *Appreciations* (London, 1889), pp. 16–17.

[4] John Killham, *Tennyson and "The Princess": Reflections of an Age* (London, 1958), p. 272.

[5] Arthur J. Carr, "Tennyson as a Modern Poet," *University of Toronto Quarterly*, XIX (July 1950), 361–382.

[6] William Butler Yeats, "Sailing to Byzantium." .

[7] William York Tindall, *Forces in Modern British Literature* (New York, 1947), pp. 94–95.

free to "surround his personal subjects with the rich trappings of myth and legend, to suffuse them with a noble and melodious melancholy, to align his psychic ambivalences with permanently affecting oppositions of the life of man and nature." [8]

In the poems of Tennyson which deal with the past, we find the same ambivalence of value and meaning that we have already noted in the tensions between retreat and return, the aesthetic retreat and the brawling world, the ascetic asylum and man's social duties, faith and doubt. The poet transplants to the safe past the suspect longings of his present state. He writes about the illustrious dead in poems which are highly autobiographical. He examines the life of the past, but through the arras he thrusts his sword into the Polonius-present which lurks in inadequate concealment there. Because of the depth of the background and the poet's freedom in concealment, Tennyson's poems of the past often make his contemporary poems seem thin by comparison. "We may hold that the thought of Tennyson is not so well bestowed in the argumentative poems . . . as in some of those where he uses mythology, the legends of *Tithonus* or the *Holy Grail*, to convey his reading of the world. The difference between the two kinds of thought is very great; and the nobler kind is not discourse but vision. It does not lend itself to discussion; if it is once apprehended there is no more to be said, or no more than the words of Sir Bors in the *Holy Grail*: 'Ask me not, for I may not speak of it, I saw it.'" [9]

Because considerable space and discussion have already been devoted to the major medieval poems—"The Lady of Shalott," "Galahad," "Morte d'Arthur," *Idylls of the King*, "Mariana"— the selection of poems from the past will be made entirely from the classical poems, often regarded as the very best Tennyson *genre*. But there is no reason to feel that the selectiveness militates against a general application of the conclusions.

[8] G. Robert Stange, "Tennyson's Mythology—a Study of 'Demeter and Persephone,'" *English Literary History*, XXI (March 1954), 68.

[9] William Paton Ker, *Tennyson*, The Leslie Stephen Lecture (Cambridge, 1909).

Attempts have often been made to distinguish the "classical" poems from Tennyson's other work, and to find in them a firmer tone, an elevated impersonality. But the fact is that every Greek or Roman theme that the poet chose to treat became in his hands a symbolic narrative of separation, either from an object of love or from the natural course of life. Such dissimilar classical poems as "Oenone," "Ulysses," and "Tithonus" share this central theme. In each case the subject offered an opportunity for a figurative expression of personal concerns, and the pattern of situation that emerges in the classical idylls is very little different from that of the poems based on history, medieval legend, or original narrative.[10]

The predominance of the theme of separation in the medieval poems that has already been noted will also again be observed in the classical poems to be considered in this chapter. Whether G. Robert Stange's contention of the centrality of the "separation" motif can be sustained in meticulous detail or not, a discussion of the classical poems certainly leads to conclusions and deals with elements typical of any other group of his poems.

"Oenone," first printed in 1833 but made less ornate and more sparely stately in the 1842 edition, describes one of Tennyson's many forsaken ladies. It is very likely that Lucas' stricture, "a painted grief upon a painted mountain,"[11] refers not only to the static quality of the poem—all moaning, no motion—but also to the odd quality of choice involved. Tennyson decides to write about the golden apple, the judgment of Paris, and the causes of the Trojan War. But, just as in "The Lotos-Eaters," he describes action through memory and life through the past. Overcast with the muted tones of melancholy, Oenone ponders her betrayal, her forsaken plight and her anticipated revenge. The whole story is told by a nymph, in tears, complaining to her "mother Ida." Oenone is one with Mariana, the lady of Shalott, the lily maid of Astalot, and the

---

[10] Stange, "Tennyson's Mythology," p. 70.
[11] Frank Laurence Lucas, *Ten Victorian Poets* (New York, 1948), p. 16.

Queen Mary about whom Lord Howard explained in Tennyson's play of the same name:

> Her life, since Philip left her, and she lost
> Her fierce desire of bearing him a child,
> Hath, like a brief and bitter winter's day,
> Gone narrowing down and darkening to a close.
>   [*Queen Mary*, IV, iii, 274–277]

She differs from them in that she gets her revenge ("The Death of Oenone," 1892), but afterward, with stark simplicity both of language and of mood, she plunges into her husband's pyre, closing a life in which she was always "led by dream and by vague desire." Tennyson so often celebrated the experience of rejection in song that both theme and mood became characteristics of his verse.

The general characteristics of Tennyson's classical poems may be noted in "Oenone." First, there is the solid groundwork of myth which has been revived in such a manner that the emotions felt by the figure of fable are poignant and moving in the nineteenth-century poem. Second, as Stange suggested, this is a poem of separation; but more than that, it is a poem of rejection and betrayal. Third, this is a poem of life confronted by impossible choices: to whom dare Paris give the golden apple? Ought any man to have to choose one from among the offerings of power, honor, self-reverence, self-knowledge, self-control, and "the most loving wife in Greece?" Tennyson strongly indicates that Paris' choice was a bad one, fraught with the promise of disastrous war and death. But it also seems that he was characteristically lining up qualities which ought not to be separated, but to each of which some measure of devotion should be given. Fourth, the tone of the poem is melancholy and the mood is one of ineffectual regret. Fifth, the solution for Oenone is mourning, revenge and death; "Dear mother Ida, harken ere I die." The memory of the good times and the hopes for future goodness never overbalance the regret that those good times are past and the sense that the only possible future is death.

Douglas Bush says that the sailors of "The Lotos-Eaters," 1832, are not "a band of tough, hairy, brine-stained Greek mariners eager for food and drink," but "a chorus of college-bred poets" making a most "delicate analysis of modern ennui." [12] The poet might have chosen many scenes of battle and sea-adventure from the *Odyssey*, but instead he chose to explore the dreamy states of consciousness of men drugged by the lotos. He chose a passage from the most renowned literature of the ancient world, but filled it full of modern tensions, modern desire to escape, and modern guilt. "*The Lotos-Eaters* is not an isolated moral holiday, its plea for selfish irresponsibility, for escape from the claims of duty and effort, is related to Tennyson's frequent personal expressions of weariness and disillusionment." [13] Again the theme of separation emerges as the drugged mariners are left to dream on the island, away from their families and the stormy sea and the civic responsibilities that ought to challenge every man. The poet evidently thinks that the choice that was made is both socially reprehensible and personally pleasant.

"The Hesperides" was published in the edition of 1833, omitted from later editions, and republished by Hallam Tennyson in the *Memoir*. [14] The poem, as a totality, defies analysis and there seems to be no complete and coherent interpretation. In the romantic tradition, it certainly adds strangeness to beauty. Its use of myth is not the traditional archetypal framework but creative to the point of myth making. The use of numbers combined with the sensuous swell and flow of the song makes it seem more of a deliberately magical incantation than a poem of description or mood. Without making a full analysis, there are certain clues to meaning which can be picked out. Jerome Buckley suggests that the sacred tree which

[12] Douglas Bush, *Mythology and the Romantic Tradition* (Cambridge, Mass., 1937), p. 207.

[13] *Ibid.*

[14] Hallam, Lord Tennyson, *Alfred, Lord Tennyson: A Memoir by His Son* (New York, 1897), I, 61.

bears the golden fruit is the aesthetic ideal; Hesper, the dragon, and the daughters are the guardians of the wellspring of pure poetry, carefully guarded and kept separate from the common lives and lore of men. [15] According to this reading, the central situation of the poem provides one more indication of the poet's desire to retreat from the common life. The mood of fearful waiting and magical formulas will one day be broken "from the East" when Hercules slays the dragon and steals the fruit. Evening both fears and hates the dawn, for Father Hesper's purple evening is the hour for poets. Day resembles "keen discovery" in "Timbuctoo" and the "terrible muses" of "Parnassus," for it dissipates the poet's hour and imperils the reign of imagination. However, it is not quite fair to say that "The Hesperides" is Tennyson's "most eloquent defense of a pure poetry isolated from the rude touch of men." [16] The golden fruit is not itself fruitful, for no poet feeds upon it. Hanno hears the sisters' song only "Till he reached the outer sea." This is a curiously sterile poetic paradise. The beauty of the poem lies in the hushed but tremulous mood of fearful waiting. The meaning of the poem will only emerge when waiting is broken by action, and the only action possible is the theft of the fruit by which "the ancient secret" will be "revealed" to men. Thus, if the song is about "pure poetry," it is poetry so pure that it is not only separated from the world of men but also from any possible audience (other than the temporarily becalmed "Zidonian Hanno"). The poet fears the moment when the aesthetic ideal is embodied in printed verse and thrust out into a critical and uncaring world. But, nevertheless, that this shall be done is the only possible climax for the poem and the only meaning for the poet. Read in this manner, the poem describes the artistic retreat, the joys the artist knows there, and the waiting which is both fearful and anticipatory of the deed which will resolve the stasis and make complete the poet's task. As

[15] Jerome Hamilton Buckley, *Tennyson: The Growth of a Poet* (Cambridge, Mass., 1960), p. 47.

[16] *Ibid.*

new science put all in doubt for John Donne, it put all in doubt and fear for Tennyson. Nevertheless he read it avidly, wrote about it frequently, heralded its necessary advances, and sought to understand its impact upon his art and the faith and future of the world. The "day" of "keen discovery" when Hercules invades the garden and the new "terrible muses" are enthroned is a time to be dreaded, yet Tennyson knows that poetry and science must engage their alien spirits in the modern world.

As Tennyson had portrayed young Greeks dreaming away their lives in "The Lotos-Eaters," ten years later, in 1842, he portrayed restless old Greeks who, refusing to "rust unburnished," set out on what might be their last voyage, under the leadership of Ulysses, known for "always roaming with a hungry heart." He returned to Homer via Dante for his source, but characteristically and cryptically he said, "There is more about myself in 'Ulysses'" [17] than in *In Memoriam*. Although we may feel like replying, "Nonsense!" at least the poet has been good enough to doff his mask momentarily and admit that his classical poem about Ulysses has a good deal to say about himself. Ulysses is not the uncomplicated Homeric voyager whose adventurous spirit is a positive good and indeed essential to bring him back to Penelope and Telemachus at Ithaca. Instead, this is the Ulysses who was placed in "The Inferno" by Dante because of his immoderate and sacrilegious desire for experience. In Canto XXVI Ulysses accuses himself of callousness to those who loved him:

> Nor fondness for my son, nor reverence
> Of my old father, nor return of love,
> That should have crown'd Penelope with joy,
> Could overcome in me the zeal I had
> To explore the world, and search the ways of life,
> Man's evil and his virtue.

A bit later in the same canto of *The Divine Comedy*, he repeats his speech to his mariners at the Strait of Gibraltar in language to which Tennyson's poem is obviously indebted:

[17] Tennyson (Hallam), *Memoir*, I, 304–305.

"O brothers!" I began, "who to the west
Through perils without number now have reach'd;
To this short remaining watch, that yet
Our senses have to wake, refuse not proof
Of the unpeopled world, following the track
Of Phoebus. Call to mind from whence ye sprang:
Ye were not form'd to live the life of brutes,
But virtue to pursue and knowledge high." [18]

W. B. Stanford suggests that in Tennyson's poem we are
hearing five voices: in addition to the voices of Homer and
Dante, the voices of Shakespeare, Byron, and Tennyson. [19] And
many critics have virtually added a sixth voice by treating this
poem as if it had been written by Robert Browning and the line
"to strive, to seek, to find, and not to yield" cribbed from
"Prospice." Let us remember that Ulysses is a grizzled hero of
the wars who has returned home but is not content to stay.
As W. H. Auden says, "refusing to be a responsible and useful
person," [20] he resigns his sovereignty over the citizens of
Ithaca to his "aged wife" Penelope and his son Telemachus,
whom he churlishly describes as

discerning to fulfill
This labor, by slow prudence to make mild
A rugged people, and thro' soft degrees
Subdue them to the useful and the good.
Most blameless is he, centred in the sphere
Of common duties. [lines 35–40]

Then at evening, the old mariners set out (lines 54–60) to experience "Life piled on life" and to follow "knowledge like a
sinking star." E. J. Chiasson was so distressed by Ulysses'
"connubial insensitivity" and "scorn for his people" that he

---

[18] Dante Alighieri, *The Divine Comedy* (New York, 1947), "The Inferno,"
Canto XXVI, lines 92–97, 109–116, p. 111. Translated by Henry F. Cary.

[19] W. B. Stanford, *The Ulysses Theme: A Study in the Adaptability of a
Traditional Hero* (Oxford, 1954), p. 202.

[20] W. H. Auden, introduction, *A Selection from the Poems of Alfred, Lord
Tennyson* (Garden City, 1944), p. xx.

claimed that Tennyson was drawing a character whom the reader was to dislike and disagree with, the "sheer incarnation of Renaissance *superbia*." [21] According to this reading, we are expected to condemn the old wanderer who evades his social responsibilities and despises his wife, son, and subjects, in order to seek more of the same kind of knowledge—experience, not wisdom—of which he has already had too much. His desire for "life piled on life" is simply the Pelion on Ossa of an old man who never really grew up.

It is doubtful whether many would agree with Chiasson's reading, but it does point out what W. W. Robson called "the dilemma of Tennyson." The incongruity of "Ulysses" may be summed up like this: "Tennyson, the responsible social being, the admirably serious and 'committed' Victorian intellectual, is uttering strenuous sentiments in the accent of Tennyson the most unstrenuous, lonely, and poignant of poets." [22] This is to say that the incongruity of the poem comes from the discrepancy between Tennyson's style and Browning's sentiments. Such a reading is undoubtedly fostered by an excerpt from the *Memoir*, stating that Tennyson had written the poem soon after the death of Arthur Hallam to express the need of "going forward and braving the struggle of life." [23] But this needs to be interpreted by a statement recorded by W. J. Rolfe. "When reading 'In Memoriam' to Mr. Knowles, the poet said: 'It is a very impersonal poem as well as personal. There is more about myself in "Ulysses," which was written under the sense of loss and that all had gone by, but that still life must be fought out to the end. It was more written with the feeling of his loss upon me than many poems in "In Memoriam".'" [24] The *Memoir*

---

[21] E. J. Chiasson, "Tennyson's 'Ulysses'—a Re-Interpretation," in John Killham (ed.), *Critical Essays on the Poetry of Tennyson* (London, 1960), pp. 155 ff.

[22] W. W. Robson, "The Dilemma of Tennyson," in John Killham (ed.), *Critical Essays*, p. 159.

[23] Tennyson (Hallam), *Memoir*, I, 196.

[24] W. J. Rolfe (ed.), *The Complete Poetical Works of Tennyson*, Cambridge Edition (Boston, 1898), p. 808 n.

quotation sounds vigorous and hopeful; the Rolfe quotation expresses only the dogged determination of a sorrowful man.

The glories of this poem, one of the most admired of the classical poems, should be apparent to all. In stately blank verse the hungry-hearted roaming of the mariner is extolled (lines 10–20). The imagery of arched experience is justly celebrated. The Stoic disregard of age and death strikes a note of amplitude and measured fearlessness. Tennyson's great love of the sea and its symbolic significance for him are expressed in incomparable phrase and image: "when / Thro' scudding drifts the rainy Hyades / Vext the dim sea"; "there gloom the dark, broad seas"; "the lights begin to twinkle from the rocks"; "the deep / Moans round with many voices"; "Smite the sounding furrows"; "the baths of all the western stars." The great appeal of the poem is, presumably, its combination of almost Augustan stateliness of diction with human gallantry and the swelling of the sea. A close reading that moves beyond the grand manner of the verse will reveal a remarkable movement of thought. The Ithaca of responsibilities is rejected in favor of ceaseless voyaging into ever widening experience. Experience is described in two ways; first as "that untravell'd world whose margin fades / For ever and for ever when I move." This kind of experience is a horizontal plane, ever more and more of the same. But second, experience may also bring "Some work of noble note. . . . Not unbecoming men that strove with Gods." The first is a kind of landscape, the second moves upward and inward to an acropolis of honor, esteem and fame. Arthur Carr points out that experience has a third transformation, when the fading margin is forsaken entirely and the plaudits of men fade into unimportance, and "It may be we shall touch the Happy Isles / And see the great Achilles, whom we knew." "Ulysses moves towards a possible reunion, as in the dream-voyage described in *In Memoriam*, section 103. . . . In small compass, Tennyson forecasts the dual answer of *In Memoriam*: life and nature are a continuum extending uninterruptedly towards a spiritual climax; yet at some point the 'lower' material world passes over into the 'higher' spiritual world. The continuum belongs to the world of nature and history; in the subjective vision of reunion with Hallam, the poet crosses the bar between two separate spheres." [25]

"Ulysses" can be arranged in a thought sequence with other poems. "The Lotos-Eaters" depicts the social evasion of retreat, "The Voyage" the evasion of endless and aimless quest, whereas "Ulysses" presents the case for a justifiable social evasion because experience may be transformed and a "newer world" found. "To Ulysses" might be read as a later (1889) and quieter recantation of even that seemingly justified social evasion. W. G. Palgrave, consul at Sonkhoum Kale, Trebizond, St. Thomas, Manila, Bulgaria, Bangkok, and Uruguay, had sent a volume of his essays entitled *Ulysses* to Tennyson. In return, the poet praised the "much-experienced" man, and at seventy-nine recalled his own youthful zeal for transcendent experience, "I, once half-crazed for larger light / On broader zones beyond the foam." He no longer tries to pile life on life, "But chaining fancy now at home," he dwells quietly "Among the quarried downs of Wight."

Lemuel Gulliver longed to see the immortal Struldbruggs, but once seen they proved to be hideous, useless, and pathetic. [26] The youthful hero of Tennyson's poem, "Tithonus," 1842, seemed "to his great heart none other than a god" when Aurora granted him the divine gift of immortality. But the immortal and aged Tithonus begs querulously,

> Let me go; take back thy gift.
> Why should a man desire in any way
> To vary from the kindly race of men. . . .
> [lines 27–29]

This same longing to be identified with mankind, to escape

[25] Carr, "Tennyson as a Modern Poet," pp. 361–382.

[26] Jonathan Swift, *The Portable Swift*, Carl Van Doren (ed.), *Travels Into Several Remote Nations of the World, by Lemuel Gulliver* (New York, 1948), Part III, Chapter 10.

isolation by participation in the common lot, even if that lot be death, may also be found in the last lines of *Maud*:

> It is better to fight for the good than to rail at the ill;
> I have felt with my native land, I am one with my kind,
> I embrace the purpose of God, and the doom assign'd.

Tithonus, son of Laomedon, king of Troy, was the husband of Aurora, goddess of the dawn. At her request the gods granted Tithonus immortality, but she neglected to ask for the gift of eternal youth, so her lover became withered and ugly and the contrast was painful between her "rosy shadows" and his "wrinkled feet." "Tithonus" is so full of the desire for death that Buckley calls "Ulysses" and "Tithonus" the "two voices of a divided sensibility."[27] In "The Grasshopper," 1830, Tennyson had mocked the legend of wrinkled Tithonus mercifully turned into a grasshopper—"No Tithon thou as poets feign. . . . No withered immortality." In "Tithonus," of which the first draft was written by the end of 1833, but which was not published until 1860, he accepts the integrity of the legend and both recreates the myth with unforgettable poignancy and fills it with his own doubts and weariness. Characteristically, the "gray shadow" mourns the youth chosen by Aurora, "so glorious in his beauty." He asks if even eternal love and beauty will not pall and become a weariness of the spirit. The imagery of the poem is highly erotic, even though this is a poem of impotence as well as of age. Much of the metrical effectiveness comes from the combination of the forthright dignity of blank verse and the emotion of a lyric, overlaid with the world-weariness of an elegy. It is a poem of separation in that, together, Tithonus and Aurora are entirely unlike, and the deepest longing of the one is to be freed from the other. It is also a poem of contrasts, the normal decay and death of the friendly earth versus the marble coldness and eternal youth and perfection of the dawn. It is one of the saddest of Tennyson's classical poems, producing a mood of high melancholy and

[27] Buckley, *Tennyson*, p. 62.

filled with memorable phrase: "after many a summer dies the swan"; "Then didst thou grant mine asking with a smile, / Like wealthy men who care not how they give"; the vivid passage in which the wild horses that love Aurora shake "the darkness from their loosen'd manes" and beat "the twilight into flakes of fire"; and the lines in which the light gently rises from a "mysterious glimmer," a reddening cheek, a brightening eye, to a "glow that slowly crimson'd all." The closing lines ache with the contrast of the eternal beauty of the gods and the tired old age of humanity:

> Thou seest all things, thou wilt see my grave;
> Thou wilt renew thy beauty morn by morn,
> I earth in earth forget these empty courts,
> And thee returning on thy silver wheels.
>
> [lines 73–76]

There is also a delightful little fragment of Tennysonian dubiety, firmly embedded in the legend but raising the old question of identity and its relationship to time: "In days far-off, and with what other eyes / I used to watch—if I be he that watch'd."

In "Lucretius," 1860, Tennyson turned from myth to history, from Greece to Rome, and in some degree, perhaps, from Tennyson to Browning and Swinburne. Lucretius is the Epicurean philosopher who wrote *De Rerum Natura* and set forth an atomic theory at the time of the breakdown of the old republic amidst the bloodbath of Sulla's proscriptions. One might expect from the poet a more austere and less lyrical treatment than "The Hesperides" or "Tithonus," but the "storm in the night" is full of the lurid flashes of lightning and the mental thunderstorms of the Spasmodics, the satyr-oread passage is reminiscent of Swinburne's exaltation of cruel passion,[28] and the hero who explains himself and confesses that the philosophy which had sustained him in the past was no longer adequate is much like Browning's long series of characters who appear in their own defense. Douglas Bush sums up the

---

[28] Sir Harold Nicolson, *Tennyson: Aspects of His Life, Character, and Poetry* (Boston, 1922), pp. 207, 230.

poem as "a very powerful picture of a noble Roman patriot who feels himself breaking along with the old republic; a Roman conscience which in its torments is more Hebraic and puritan than Greek; a Roman intellect which has sought with passionate honesty for the truth that delivers from evil and fear; a prophet and preacher of serenity whose creed has failed him; a poet and philosopher whose joy in nature has turned to ashes." [29] Buckley noted the ambivalence of the poem that both appreciates *De Rerum Natura* and indicates the inadequacy of even the most heroic materialism. [30] There are some important similarities between "Lucretius" and Matthew Arnold's *Empedocles on Etna*, 1852. The "name characters" in both poems were publicists of atomism, both expressed a distrust of the high gods and a noble reliance on their own strength of character, both were overwhelmed by qualities they had hardly considered in their philosophies, both ended in suicide.

In Tennyson's blank verse poem, Lucretius is married to a much younger woman, Lucilia, who finds him so cold and unresponsive that she is not sure she is really loved. He drinks a love philter she has prepared, which, "tickling the brute brain within the man's," makes him loathe himself. On the following stormy night, he is prey in dreams to all the forces he has hitherto held back by self-control, intellectual power, and nobility of character. A lightning flash breaks the continuity of nature, reducing all to the atoms to which he himself had reduced nature in his philosophy. The orgies of blood and vice which he had always avoided in the Rome of Sulla take place in a circle about him, narrowing closer until he cries aloud. Then he sees the breasts of Helen of Troy menaced by a threatening sword, and the fire that shoots out of them scorches not only the "roofless Ilion" but the dreaming Lucretius as well. He asks if this has come to him because of his neglect of Venus and thus is led to the thought of the gods and how impossible it is that they can exist in an atom-composed universe, but the

[29] Bush, *Mythology*, p. 214.
[30] Buckley, *Tennyson*, p. 166.

philter makes his great mind break down: "I have forgotten what I meant; my mind / Stumbles, and all my faculties are lamed." Apollo of the sun, with all his light, cannot tell whether the philosopher means to take his life before the close of day. Lucretius ponders Plato's counsel that like a soldier he must not quit his post until relieved. But he is overwhelmed in his noble thoughts by a hideous company like the horrors of a painting by Hieronymus Bosch, "prodigies of myriad naked-nesses, / And twisted shapes of lust, unspeakable, / Abominable." Nature is "nobler from her bath of storm"; cannot the philos-opher throw off the memory of the horrors of his dreams? But even waking he seems to see a charming oread with "slippery sides, / And rosy knees and supple roundedness, / And budded bosom-peaks" pursued by a satyr. Lucretius hates, abhors, spits, sickens at him, yet hears himself cry, "Catch her, goat-foot!" and when she is caught, he first begs the myrtles and laurels to hide them and then asks, "do I wish . . . that the bush were leafless?" And so because some "unseen monster lays / His vast and filthy hands" upon his will, Lucretius determines to die and leave the life that gave him joy only in "shutting reasons up in rhythm . . . to make a truth less harsh," a life of which he "often grew / Tired." Then, much like Empedocles, he commends his body to the universal atoms to be reshaped in nature's economy as a bird, beast, fish, flower, or man. But man himself may not have long on this earth before all things break down and atoms pass into the void. Then, as Stopford Brooke wrote, "he dies rather than be mastered by lustful visions which a Greek . . . would have gone through, smiled at, and forgotten . . . it takes a great poet to assimilate, as Tennyson does, the essence of Lucretius as a thinker and a poet in the space of about three hundred lines; and to combine this with the representation of a man in an hour of doom and madness. . . . Tennyson's masterly reticence, rigid restraint only to the absolutely necessary, are supreme in this poem." [31]

[31] Stopford A. Brooke, *Tennyson: His Art and Relation to Modern Life* (New York, 1899), pp. 136–137.

Many of the qualities of "Oenone" are operative in "Lucretius." The dilemma of the ancient philosopher who had created a philosophy inadequate at two extremes—carnal passion and immortality—was very real to Tennyson. So he fills a historical drama with current and personal anxieties. Again this is a poem of separation: the estrangement of an old thinker and a young wife, the dichotomy in a philosophy of thought and the life of feeling, and finally the physical separation of suicide. The poem also arrives at the solution of death, which the philosopher considers more manly than the life he has been leading—"Why should I, beastlike as I find myself, / Not manlike end myself?" This is also a poem of choice, the choice of an unsuitable wife, the choice of an intellectual naturalism which bars sexual passion, the choice of death with honor rather than life without. And like the judgment of Paris, such a choice ought never to have to be made. The Roman poet-philosopher should have made room in his philosophy of self-control for the passions that link us to the beasts and the worship that unites us with the gods. The mood is unusual in that the customary muted melancholy of stasis is replaced by lurid dreams, a stormy nature, and a violent deed.

In the spring of 1879, Tennyson's favorite brother, Charles Turner, died. The summer of 1880 found Alfred Tennyson, in Italy for his health, visiting the site of Catullus' villa at Sirmione, reached by boat from Desenzano. With thoughts perhaps returning to the death of his own brother,[32] he recalls the Roman poet's lament on the death of his brother, and once again the ancient past becomes a commentary on the moods and longings of the Victorian poet. Separation of death is in both the past and the present, and the separation of an island from the mainland underlines its loneliness. The title of the poem, "*Frater Ave Atque Vale*," quotes the end of Catullus' refrain. In nine lines of iambic octometer, all rhyming on the open vowel "o,"[33] an exceedingly difficult form is mastered:

[32] Bush, *Mythology*, p. 226.
[33] Nicolson, *Tennyson: Aspects*, pp. 285–286.

"Row us out from Desenzano, to your Sirmione row!" There are "purple flowers" of death and a "Poet's hopeless woe," but there is also the solace of the beauty of nature—the "summer glow" and "the Lydian laughter of the Garda Lake below." The living poet mourning a dead brother-poet writes about a Roman poet mourning his dead brother-poet. Tennyson, like Catullus, was comforted by the beauty of landscape and poetry. The separation of death is alleviated in the nineteenth century A.D., as in the first century B.C., by memory and art.

Douglas Bush called Tennyson's "To Virgil," 1882,

. . . the briefest and finest appreciation of Virgil ever written, and it is, indirectly, the best possible testimony to the nature of Tennyson's Virgilian inspiration. He also is a landscape-lover, a lord of language, he is, at moments, majestic in his sadness at the doubtful doom of human kind, and for him hope gleams like a golden branch amid the shadows . . . both . . . had absorbed a rich literary culture, and were the most scholarly and ornate stylists of their age. . . . Their best work is essentially elegiac, the product of a temperamental melancholy, a brooding, wistful sense of the past, an unappeasable *desiderium* which is deepened by troubled questionings about the present and the future.[34]

In an unusual form of ten quatrains of alternating iambic tetrameter and pentameter lines, rhyming a b c b, Tennyson hymned his admiration for the poet to whom he had often been compared and with whom he felt a self-conscious kinship. Written at the request of the Mantuans for the nineteenth centenary of Virgil's death, Tennyson recalls in quatrain I the topics of the *Aeneid*, in quatrains II and III the *Georgics*, and certain of the *Eclogues* in quatrains IV–VII. The Victorian poet invites comparison when he calls Virgil "Landscape-lover, lord of language. . . . All the chosen coin of fancy flashing out from many a golden phrase," the poet of the "lonely word," the prophet "majestic in thy sadness at the doubtful doom of human kind." Certainly he shared the workman's passion of

[34] Bush, *Mythology*, p. 226.

"Old Virgil who would write ten lines, they say, / At dawn, and lavish all the golden day / To make them wealthier in his readers' eyes." [35]

"It appears that, in point of style, poets may be divided into two main classes: those who believe that first thoughts are best, and those who hold that retouching is a part of inspiration . . . the distinction which included Shakespeare among the poets who never blotted a line and Virgil among those who were content to spend the whole day in polishing a short passage points to a real cleavage of temperament and method." [36] In the foregoing quotation, Bernard Groom was using Virgil to illustrate the "traditional style" in letters, of which Tennyson was the nineteenth-century exponent. Love of landscape, lordship of language, the careful labor of the polisher of phrases, a majestic sadness in view of the doubtful doom of human kind—these qualities link Virgil and Tennyson and are as good a description of one as of the other. Tennyson paints a fair likeness of Virgil, but the portrait might equally well be entitled "Portrait of the Artist," for the Roman poet was one with whom Tennyson had often been compared and the qualities of love of nature, linguistic craftsmanship and overarching sadness are the very qualities for which he is admired. Thus old and new, past and present, merge and become one.

"Tiresias," first published in 1885, had been written much earlier, as we learn from the dedicatory poem "To E. Fitz-Gerald": "my son, who dipt / In some forgotten book of mine / With sallow scraps of manuscript, / And dating many a year ago, / Has hit on this." The figure of the blind prophet pleading with Menoeceus, son of Creon and a direct descendant of Cadmus, to sacrifice himself in order to save Thebes, bears many resemblances to Tennyson himself. At several periods of his life, the poet was convinced that he was in imminent danger of losing his sight. In 1884 he wrote with special sympathy to a

[35] "Old Poets Foster'd Under Friendlier Skies," 1885.
[36] Bernard Groom, "On the Diction of Tennyson, Browning and Arnold," *Society for Pure English*, Tract LIII (Oxford, 1939), 94.

blind servant, Susan Epton, and to a blind Sheffield blacksmith; and he confessed to Francisque Michel, "my eyes are failing and I fear that I may be slowly growing blind." [37] This is a strange fulfillment for the elderly poet who in youth had assumed the role of a blind, old prophet.

Like Tiresias, doomed by the unforgiving gods "to speak the truth that no man may believe," Tennyson must often have felt out of step with an age in which science grew and beauty dwindled, [38] and certainly sometimes he felt that he had lived "a very useless life." [39] As he accused himself in the second *Locksley Hall*—"I myself have often babbled doubtless of a foolish past"—he begins "Tiresias" with the blind, aged prophet wishing he were "as in the years of old." As Tiresias had been struck blind because he had "seen too much," perhaps Tennyson felt that his vision of the world was too deep, too critical for an age which desired uncritical anthems of praise. Tennyson had had much opportunity to observe in his own time that the "tyranny of one / Was prelude to the tyranny of all" and that the tyranny of all in turn led backward "to the tyranny of one." Like Wordsworth in *The Convention of Cintra*, Tennyson noted with somewhat less disillusionment that the revolutionary liberator, after a brief period of anarchic democracy, then becomes the tyrant dictator. The poet rebukes himself as he dreams that people will esteem him for the "boundless yearning of the prophet's heart" when he knows full well that "virtue must shape itself in deed." In urging Menoeceus to self-sacrifice he develops a cluster of meanings. First, a youth is asked to suffer for something in which he had no personal part in order to appease the irresponsible whim of the gods. Second, a youth is counseled to take his whole life and pack it into one splendid, never-to-be-forgotten deed. Third, he offers to life the solution of death. Fourth, he urges a high-minded youth to achieve that magnanimity of compassion that

---

[37] Tennyson (Hallam), *Memoir*, II, 304, 311.
[38] *Locksley Hall Sixty Years After*.
[39] Tennyson (Hallam), *Memoir*, II, 337.

sacrifices personal life for civic weal. All of these are themes integral to the thought and vision of the Poet Laureate. As Lucretius "often grew / Tired of so much within our little life," and Tiresias sighed, "I would that I were gather'd to my rest," Tennyson grew progressively weary with a world in which the wise man's word is trampled underfoot by the populace, a world from which, as he states in *Locksley Hall Sixty Years After*,

All I loved are vanish'd voices, all my steps are on the dead.
All the world is ghost to me, and as the phantom disappears,
Forward far and far from here is all the hope of eighty years.
(lines 252–254)

In the epilogue, in which the poet writes about the death of FitzGerald, Tennyson himself enunciates the modernity of the classical poems: "And mixt the dream of classic times, / And all the phantoms of the dream, / With present grief." Once again the poet wrestles with the question of immortality, which for him is question still, by stating the characteristic "If": If FitzGerald, dying, went out into a "deeper night" than this world's "poor twilight," then it is "barren toil" to exist and no life "so maim'd by night" is worth "our living out," surely not "mine to me."

Again this is a poem of separation—sight from eyes, life from a youth, prophet from his people; a poem of terrifying choice— my life or the existence of my city; a poem of great world-weariness and the solution of death.

Hallam Tennyson said that "Demeter and Persephone," 1889, was written at his request, because he knew that his father considered Demeter "one of the most beautiful types of womanhood." [40] But Tennyson should have needed no filial prompting to be interested by a myth in which light alternates with darkness and life with death, and in which two kinds of love provide two different clues to identity, and the extremes of heaven and hell reveal a curious kinship. Robert Stange suggests that Tennyson's interest was less in "one of the most

[40] *Ibid.*, p. 364.

beautiful types of womanhood" than in "the scheme of related antinomies from which the imagery of the poem develops, and which are inherent in the myth." [41] Demeter is a meaningful type of womanhood to Tennyson because her love triumphs over the power of death, although only in partial victory. The "mother's childless cry . . . rang thro' Hades, Earth, and Heaven" until

> Rain-rotten died the wheat, the leaf fell, and the Sun,
> Pale at my grief, drew down before his time
> Sickening, and Aetna kept her winter snow.
>
> [lines 110–112]

The poet too had known bitterest loss; for him too the earth had seemed "a fruitless fallow" and "man, that only lives and loves an hour, / Seem'd nobler than" the "hard eternities" of the gods. The life of Persephone becomes neither darkness nor light, neither life nor death, but "nine white moons" on the earth, wrapped in the love of her mother, and "Three dark ones in the shadow" with her king. Which is Persephone's real love—filial or passional, φιλία or ἔρως; which was her real home—earth or Hades; which was her real identity—daughter or wife; which was the source of richer experience, to share with Pluto, philosophers and poets the vision of

> those imperial, disimpassion'd eyes
>
> .   .   .   .
>
> That oft had seen the serpent-wanded power
> Draw downward into Hades with his drift
> Of flickering spectres [lines 23, 25–27]

or to walk the field of Enna, ablaze with flowers that brighten as her footsteps fall? Tennyson's Persephone is not just the "human-godlike" child of Demeter, she is also the wife of Pluto and the Queen of Death; innocence and experience are united and each is loth to let the other go. Persephone is far more than the pathetic stolen maid of Greek myth; by her

---

[41] Stange, "Tennyson's Mythology," p. 71.

abduction and the loving darkness that holds her she has become one with Tiresias, Lucretius, Merlin, and the Ancient Sage, to whom have been given visions of deep and secret wisdom at the price of danger and terror to themselves and to their world.

The most disheartening discovery of the mourning mother is the kinship of the highest to the lowest. The abduction of Persephone is not simply an evil act of the prince of evil, but it is permitted by his brother, who is the king of heaven. Thus heaven and hell are not in their usual simple relationship of hostility, but rather in the highly philosophical and deeply permanent one of brotherhood, unity, identity. It is as if Tennyson were saying to the grieving mother, "Despite all your grief and all your love, the tension between life and death remains, and the best you can know is alternating periods of each." Perhaps he thus shared the wisdom experience had brought to him. In a world ruled by the brothers of heaven and hell, only half the fulfillment of desire is possible. Death will be half conquered and sorrow only half consoled.

When Hallam requested a poem based on the Demeter-Persephone myth, his father replied: "I will write it, but when I write an antique like this I must put it into a frame—something modern about it. It is no use giving a mere *réchauffé* of old legends." [42] At this point, Tennyson states the argument of this chapter. It is no use to warm over old legends. They must relate to modern life and current needs. The past is of eternal fascination to the poet, but he will yield to its allure only when his conscience is satisfied that in re-creating the past he is contributing something of significance to the present. Having paid tribute to the two tensions of time, he went on to state that the "frame" was the following passage:

> Yet I, Earth-Goddess, am but ill-content
> With them who still are highest. Those gray heads,
> What meant they by their "Fate beyond the Fates"
> But younger kindlier Gods to bear us down,

[42] Tennyson (Hallam), *Memoir*, II, 364.

As we bore down the Gods before us? Gods,
To quench, not hurl the thunderbolt, to stay,
Not spread the plague, the famine; Gods indeed,
To send the noon into the night and break
The sunless halls of Hades into Heaven?
Till thy dark lord accept and love the Sun,
And all the Shadow die into the Light.

[lines 126–136]

It can readily be seen that Tennyson's "frame" for the
Demeter and Persephone legend is far more than decorative
outline. It arises out of his own experience of separation and
heaven-questioning sorrow and provides an apocalyptic
dénouement for the poem.

When Demeter discovered from the God of dreams that
"'The Bright one in the highest / Is brother of the Dark one in
the lowest'" and that heaven and hell have connived in the
theft of her daughter and have agreed that she will be "for
evermore / The Bride of Darkness," she "cursed the Gods of
heaven" and scorned to "mingle with their feasts." A *modus
vivendi* appropriate to this world of compromise is accepted—
Persephone will dwell nine months with her mother and three
with her husband. Although accepted, such a compromise is
not acceptable to Demeter's maternal and possessive love. So
Tennyson adds to the Olympian gods and the Fates what
Shelley had added in *Prometheus Unbound* and Keats in *Hyperion*
—a great prophecy of the coming of "kindlier Gods" who will
"quench" the thunderbolt and "stay" the plague and famine
until the sun sends its light into Hades and even Pluto accepts
the priority of sorrowing love. In more personal language, if
separation and tension are the normal experiences of this world,
what is left for hope? Simply and climactically this: the powers
which rule this arbitrary world shall some day be superseded
by kindlier deities who will place love upon heaven's throne,
and thus, upon the throne of the earth. This is a surprising
climax to emerge from the elegant diction and the almost Pre-
Raphaelite imagery of this sad, shadowy drama—the more

usual mood of Tennyson's poetry.[43] In the victory of the Olympians over the Titans and the promise of the victory of Christ,[44] even the divine governance of the universe has been made subject to the law of progress. And as the heavens change, Persephone will change from the Queen of Death worshipped in fear, through reunion with her Earth-mother, to a queen of life who is worshipped in love (ἀγάπη). Most personal of all, the reference to the "souls of men, who grew beyond their race, / And made themselves as Gods against the fear / Of Death and Hell" is a clear echo of the Hallam who in *In Memoriam* was the herald of the race to come, a model of the "Christ that is to be."

When Alfred Tennyson was twenty-four he wrote a poem which was richly revelatory of his divided state then and curiously prophetic of his future development. In "Youth," written in 1833, but never published except in Hallam Tennyson's *Memoir*,[45] Part I of the poem shows a boy torn between boyhood's identification with nature and manhood's separate self-identification, called by the future to "Come along," and by the past to "Come back, come back," and saddened as that which seemed to be the permanent became the transient. In the second part, the boy who was left sitting among "scentless flowers" simply watching "the world revolve," hears a third voice which does not invite but sternly commands "Come." This is the voice of participation, of action, of work and deed, "An energy, an agony, / A labour working to an end." And so he joins the ranks of the active life amidst burning fortresses, heroic songs, tempests, the groans of men, and his "heart is dark, but yet I come." Then Love glitters through the rain and shines upon a purified world, bringing back to the man all that was sweet to the boy in the past. The clouds unwind and the man who loves catches a glimpse of the "Gods / Ray'd round with beams of living light."

[43] Stange, "Tennyson's Mythology," p. 75.
[44] John Milton, "On the Morning of Christ's Nativity."
[45] Tennyson (Hallam), *Memoir*, I, 112.

The boy of the poem was torn between past and future, just as the poet was torn. In maturity he hears the stern command, no longer invitation, to participate in life's daily warfare, and like the poet, he fulfills his societal duty. But amidst the destruction of old citadels of faith and the groans of expendable men, he longs, as does the poet, for something more tinged with the ideal, more lasting, purified, and glorious. Then Love comes after the rain, and, uniting the best of past and future, grants a vision to man of the purposes of the most high gods.

When Tennyson was twenty-four he heard the siren voice of the past sing seductively "Come back, come back" ("Youth"). When at thirty-eight he wandered amidst "happy autumn-fields," the sadness of the past—"days that are no more" ("Tears, Idle Tears")—was still regnant over his spirit. At fifty-two, the leaping streams of the Valley of Cauteretz were hushed by "the voice of the dead" ("In the Valley of Cauteretz"). The voice of the past always had great power over the poet, but it was never the only voice he heard. In "Youth," he heard the future call "Come along, come along"; he obeyed the stern command to play his part in the stirring events of his day; he felt the sweet persuasion of love and caught a glimpse of the central meaning of the universe. In "Tears, Idle Tears," the past becomes the present and death mingles contemporaneously with life. In "In the Valley of Cauteretz" the voice of the dead was not simply past and gone, but became "a living voice to me." So the voices of the poet are and remain multiple: past, present, and future; death and life; the restoration of love; and the hope of divine purpose. In Spedding's terms, a poet has been delineated who is "discontented with the present," who "yearns toward . . . and worships . . . the past," but who would be "discontented" if the past remained only the past.

V

Delicacy versus Strength

Some of the contemporaries who were introduced to Tennyson sensed his uneasy combination of strength and vigor of body along with delicacy and sensitivity of spirit. Thus this chapter explores the "Apollo-Hercules" combination of his personality, the "Camilla-Ajax" combination of his style, and the feminine-masculine *personae* of his poems. This exploration notes the frequency of the theme of the high-born maiden and the spurned male, and attempts to define and differentiate the ambiguity, ambivalence, paradox, and dubiety of his thought.

It was the Reverend W. H. Brookfield, to whom Tennyson addressed the sonnet of 1869, who coined the "Apollo-Hercules" phrase: "It is not fair, Alfred, that you should be Hercules as well as Apollo." [1] Tennyson was fond of long walks and "putting the stone," and on one occasion, recalled by Mrs. Lloyd of Louth, "in proof of his strong muscular power, when showing us a little pet pony on the lawn at Somersby one day, he surprised us by taking it up and carrying it." [2] It must have been one of these bucolic exhibitions that caused Brookfield to call his friend a Hercules in strength as well as an Apollo in poetry. The Right Honorable W. E. H. Lecky expressed the same reaction from a different point of view: "his sensitiveness seemed to me curiously out of harmony with his large powerful frame, with his manly dark colouring, with his great massive hands and strong square-tipped fingers." [3] It

[1] Hallam, Lord Tennyson, *Alfred, Lord Tennyson: A Memoir by His Son* (New York, 1897), I, 76.
[2] *Ibid.*
[3] *Ibid.*, II, 204.

was to be expected that such a reaction would be felt in an age which assumed that spiritual tendencies would exhibit physical evidences, but modern critics have shared the same sense of "disharmony." Sir Harold Nicolson expressed it in the description, "the virgin spirit in a Titan's form," [4] in which the virginal quality did not refer to chastity, although it well could have, but to something shy, retiring, and fearful which fluttered tremulously in his giant frame. It is natural that a raw country lad, son of a rejected first-born son, would be grateful for social acceptance by brilliant young men of more assured breeding. But perhaps, too, it was the shy spirit in a big body that made him need a friend like Arthur Henry Hallam, who could give him confidence, lead him out of his dark moods, and balance his recessive temperament with the vigor of normality.

Although Brookfield and Lecky noted the uneasy combination of sensitive massiveness, and Nicolson stressed the "virgin spirit", which was, after all, only half of a two-way tension, many friends and critics underlined "the Titan form." T. E. Welby, in *A Study of Swinburne*, commented that few of the eminent Victorians were really as tame as they seemed, for "even their typical poet, Tennyson, if you considered him closely, when he was off duty, had in him, at any rate as a man, something farouche and acrid." [5] F. L. Lucas, with his delight in stories that delineate character, reluctantly relegated to a footnote the poet's comment on Browning's intricate and obscure *Sordello*, that he understood only the first line ("Who will, may hear Sordello's story told.") and the last line ("Who would has heard Sordello's story told.") and that both were lies; also his philosophic resignation to the marriage of Jane Welsh and Thomas Carlyle since it was better two people should be miserable than four; as well as his description of the critic Churton Collins as a "louse on the locks of literature." [6]

[4] Sir Harold Nicolson, *Tennyson: Aspects of His Life, Character, and Poetry* (Boston, 1922), p. 57.

[5] T. E. Welby, *A Study of Swinburne* (New York, 1926), pp. 30–31.

[6] Frank Laurence Lucas, *Tennyson* (London, 1957), p. 14 n.

Hallam Tennyson's *Memoir* preserves Tennyson's letter to R. M. Milnes in which he refuses to send a contribution to Lord Northampton's "charity book of poetry for the destitute family of a man of letters," in a figure which is neither elegant nor delicate—"To write for people with prefixes to their names is to milk he-goats; there is neither honour nor profit." [7] With admirable forthrightness, to an acquaintance who kept assuring him that it was the greatest honor of his life to have met him, Tennyson finally replied, "'Don't talk d——d nonsense.'" [8] Such was his physical vigor that when he was eighty-two he liked to challenge his friends to get up twenty times quickly from a low chair without touching it with their hands, meanwhile performing the feat himself. [9]

Thomas Carlyle's word-pictures of the poet are almost as well known as any artist's portraits. In a letter to Ralph Waldo Emerson in America, Carlyle described Tennyson as "one of the finest looking men in the world. A great shock of rough dusky dark hair; bright, laughing, hazel eyes; massive aquiline face, most massive yet most delicate; of sallow brown complexion, almost Indian looking, clothes cynically loose, free-and-easy, smokes infinite tobacco. His voice is musical, metallic, fit for loud laughter and piercing wail, and all that may lie between: speech and speculation free and plenteous; I do not meet in these late decades such company over a pipe!" [10] While this is a thoroughly masculine portrait, we note the description of a face which was "most delicate" as well as "most massive," and of a voice which could "wail" and sing as well as laugh loudly. On September 5, 1840, for his brother John, Carlyle sketched another portrait of Tennyson—"a fine, large-featured, dim-eyed, bronze-coloured shaggy-headed man is Alfred; dusty, smoky, free and easy; who swims, outwardly and inwardly, with great composure in an articulate element as of tranquil chaos and tobacco-smoke; great now and then

[7] Tennyson (Hallam), *Memoir*, I, 158.
[8] *Ibid.*, p. 264.
[9] *Ibid.*, II, 384. [10] *Ibid.*, I, 187.

when he does emerge; a most restful, brotherly, solid-hearted man." [11] On December 7, 1842, after reading the new two-volume *Poems*, Carlyle wrote to Tennyson, "truly it is long since in any English Book, Poetry or Prose, I have felt the pulse of a real man's heart as I do in this same. A right valiant, true fighting, victorious heart; strong as a lion's, yet gentle, loving and full of music: what I call a genuine singer's heart! there are tones as of the nightingale; low murmurs as of wood-doves at summer noon; everywhere a noble sound as of the free winds and leafy woods." [12] Although Carlyle obviously felt the dual nature of the poet, it did not for him detract from the lion's heart that it was also gentle and loving, or make Tennyson seem less noble a singer because his tones were those of the nightingale or the wood-dove as well as of the free wind blowing through a leafy wood. In 1851, with his irresistible weakness for the strong epithet, he described Tennyson to Sir John Simeon as "sitting on a dung-heap among innumerable dead dogs," by which he merely meant to indicate the poet's choice of antique subjects for his poems. When Tennyson teased him about the image, he freely replied, "Eh! that was not a very luminous description of you." [13] Rich and gothic as these word-portraits were, Carlyle could not quite bury the poet beneath the life-guardsman, even if he so desired.

The Introduction to this study referred to what F. L. Lucas called "the double character of Tennyson." In two highly rhetorical paragraphs Lucas establishes the same tension that was notable in the descriptions cited above:

. . . the impressive Tennyson, tall, gypsy-dark, often as unkempt as his style was polished, strikingly handsome in youth, awesome as a Hebrew prophet in his bearded age, young Hercules who tossed iron bars over haystacks, or carried ponies 'round lawns, who seemed to FitzGerald "a sort of Hyperion," to Carlyle "a life-guardsman spoilt by making poetry," and to Sydney Dobell a figure capable of composing the *Iliad* itself; with senses so vivid that he could hear a bat shriek, though

[11] *Ibid.*, p. 189 n.   [12] *Ibid.*, p. 213.   [13] *Ibid.*, p. 340.

myopic, glimpse the moon reflected in a nightingale's eye; with such vitality that even at seventy-seven he had not a grey hair in his mane, yet often gruff and formidable, liking his meat in wedges, his tea in bowls, his tobacco in two-gallon jars, enjoying clay pipes, public-house port, broad stories; often grim in his humour, so that he would shake with sardonic laughter in reading his own St. Simeon or indulge in strange impersonations of the toad-shaped Satan whispering in the ear of Eve, or a cannibal chief inspecting edible missionaries; Johnsonian, at times, in his ruthless downrightness; yet, like Johnson, noble, generous, compassionate amid his melancholia.

But with this Tennyson there was coupled a strange sort of anti-self—shy, self-conscious, hysterical, as hypersensitive to criticism as the legendary princess to the pea beneath the mattresses, the "school miss Alfred" of Lytton's satire and of verse like "The Darling Room". . . .[14]

It is illuminating that Lucas should compare the formidable but hypersensitive Tennyson to the downright but melancholy Samuel Johnson. The lexicographer-poet-essayist, who wrote prayers full of a shuddering fear of death, was described by Louis Kronenberger as:

. . . a scarred and sick and deeply melancholy man . . . painfully aware of how far he fell short of perfect virtue, and [who] dreaded the thought that at the Judgment Day he might be held to have fallen too far short. . . . "The better a man is, the more afraid he is of death, having a clearer view of infinite purity." God, for Johnson, was someone not to love but to fear; no man ever got less comfort from his faith, or more perturbation.

In the famous colloquy with Dr. Adams there was no talking for effect; Johnson meant literally what he said. "I am afraid," he remarked, "I may be one of those who shall be damned." "What do you mean," inquired Adams, "by being damned?" "Sent to Hell, Sir," Johnson thundered back, "and punished everlastingly." Johnson's morbid horror of death was certainly as much founded on the idea of damnation as on the idea of

14 Lucas, *Tennyson*, p. 13.

dissolution. His sort of believer could hardly help being his sort of bigot.[15]

It hardly needs to be said that Johnson's writing was enriched and his life given added dimensions because, although he was fearless of men, he was fearful of God. Similarly, were Tennyson only a Hyperion, a life-guardsman, he would be less of a man than the "double-character" Lucas describes, and certainly less of a writer. It was out of this delicacy-strength tension that he wrote with an exquisite sensitiveness which yet was always masculine, a lyric line which still had virility, a sentimentality which often deepened into passion. When Algernon Charles Swinburne dogmatized that "great poets are bisexual" (in his appreciation of Tennyson's "Rizpah"),[16] it is possible that he had in mind not only the ability to see and feel as both man and woman, but also the qualities of Tennyson's style which expressed both viewpoints.

It was William Paton Ker, in the Leslie Stephen Lecture for 1909, who pointed out that Tennyson was "fond of rendering Ajax and Camilla in the movement of his line,"[17] referring, of course, to Alexander Pope's *Essay on Criticism*, and particularly to the passage:

'Tis not enough no harshness gives offence,
The sound must seem an Echo to the sense:
Soft is the strain when Zephyr gently blows,
And the smooth stream in smoother numbers flows;
But when loud surges lash the sounding shore,
The hoarse, rough verse should like the torrent roar:
When Ajax strives some rock's vast weight to throw,
The line too labours, and the words move slow;
Not so, when swift Camilla scours the plain,
Flies o'er th' unbending corn, and skims along the main.
                                    [II, lines 364–373]

[15] Louis Kronenberger (ed.), *The Portable Johnson & Boswell* (New York, 1955), pp. 8 ff.

[16] Algernon Charles Swinburne, *Miscellanies* (London, 1895), p. 221.

[17] William Paton Ker, *Tennyson*, The Leslie Stephen Lecture (Cambridge, 1909).

To illustrate Tennyson's adherence to Pope's rules, Ker quoted
two lines from "Geraint and Enid." "This is Ajax:—'He felt
were she the prize of bodily force' . . . this is Camilla, a little
retarded:—'But while the sun yet beat a dewy blade.'" While
more striking illustrations could be found in the *Idylls of the
King*, of the line that labors and the line that skims, in this
chapter, the "Camilla-Ajax of his style" is extended to include
the broader areas of general manner of treatment and choice
of topic.

In the *Quarterly*, April 1833, John Wilson Croker reviewed
the poems of 1832 as the most recent and feeblest work of "the
Cockney School." Exposed to particular ridicule was "O
Darling Room," which, in any case, is difficult to defend.
Arthur Hallam thought it was "mighty pleasant," but most
modern critics would agree with Croker in substance if not in
tone. A giggle is the only appropriate response to the effusive-
ness of "Dear room, the apple of my sight" with its repeated
refrain:

> A little room so exquisite,
> With two such couches soft and white,
> Not any room so warm and bright,
> Wherein to read, wherein to write,

to say nothing of the required pronunciation of "exquisite."
Buckley was sufficiently embarrassed by the poem to advance
the lame and quite unverifiable explanation that it should
"be regarded as a failure at humorous verse rather than an
unsuccessful and bathetic serious lyric." [18] At any rate, the discarded and uncollected poem is a particularly lush representative of a tendency which was not completely discarded in later
work and which undoubtedly invited the criticisms of "precious" and "effeminate" in the reviews of the 1842 volume. The
poet himself was quite conscious of this tendency and exposed
it to self-criticism as early as 1830, when he wryly described a

[18] Jerome Hamilton Buckley, *Tennyson: the Growth of a Poet* (Cambridge,
Mass., 1960), p. 286, notes.

"sensitive" mind as "second-rate," cloaked only by the protective "Supposed" before the descriptive phrase "Confessions of. . . ."[19]

But if "O Darling Room" is the extreme representative in his poetry of delicacy of style and manner, there are also representatives of what Nicolson called the "broad rustic humour"[20] of the Tennyson rectory tribe. "Northern Farmer, Old Style," 1864, depicts in very broad north-country dialect an earthy old man who had faced the seasons and the contrarieties of crops and flocks for forty years. Now that he is ill, neither doctor nor nurse is able to divorce him from his "point o' aale ivry noight" and his "quart ivry market-noight." "It is a vivid piece out of the great comedy of man, not of its mere mirth, but of that elemental humorousness of things which belongs to the lives of the brutes as well as to ourselves, that steady quaintness of the ancient earth and all who are born of her, which first made men smile, and which has enabled us to bear our pain better, and to love one another more, than might appear possible in a world where Nature generally seems to be doing her best to hurt us first, and then to kill us."[21] "Northern Farmer, New Style," 1870, is still in dialect but the social scale has changed. A prosperous farmer, whose horses' hooves click "proputty, proputty, proputty," is almost as good as the old Squire and better than a landless cleric. As he married for money, the farmer urges his son Sam to forget the parson's pretty but penniless daughter, for beauty fades and gentility buys no bread, but property and money last and grow. Besides recording a change in the economy of rural England, the poem records the poet's insight into an inelegant but practical and solid point of view. Both earthy and unromantic, the two poems reveal an ease with common things and an understanding of life that is far removed from darling rooms, dreams of fair women, and idylls of a long dead king. "The Northern

[19] "Supposed Confessions of a Second-Rate Sensitive Mind."
[20] Nicolson, *Tennyson, Aspects*, p. 43.
[21] Stopford A. Brooke, *Tennyson: His Art and Relation to Modern Life* (London, 1894), p. 443.

Cobbler" of 1880 underscores the same empathy with crude lives and domestic trials that are rather boastfully dramatized. There is sentiment in the sketch of Sally, but only valor and honesty in regard to "tha bottle a'stanning theer." In many ways these three dialect poems are better "English Idylls" than most of the poems listed under that title in the various editions. One which was so listed, not in dialect but broad in humor and penetratingly honest in wit, is "Will Waterproof's Lyrical Monologue, Made at the Cock" of 1842. In octaves alternately of tetrameter and trimeter, rhyming a b a b c d c d, Will begins as a self-conscious poet sentimentally recalling the lips he once had kissed and the friendships of his college years, passes through a stage of loud carousing and untethered musing, and of being "maudlin-moral," to a final invocation, not of the muse, but of a serviceable and apotheosized head-waiter. The romantic and antiromantic tendencies of the poet are equally observable, but the major tendency is toward debunking a lofty poetic aestheticism.

"Amphion," first printed in 1842, has in it this same wry tendency, as the English poet recalls the effectiveness of Amphion's song,

> Wherever he sat down and sung
> He left a small plantation;
> [lines 19–20]

but in the modern world a poet is revered neither by men nor nature. The only muses he hears are his old-maid neighbors as they read aloud some treatises on gardening—enough to make any poet decide to forget about rhyming, till his acres, and accept his lot as he finds it. Again this poem is highly anti-romantic and even antiscientific in its satirical conclusion.

Even *Enoch Arden*, 1864, contains a subtle combination of romanticism and antiromanticism. Tennyson's manuscript note indicates that the story of *Enoch Arden* came to him from Woolner the sculptor.[22] Having thus received the salty, fish-smelling

[22] Tennyson (Hallam), *Memoir*, II, 7.

tale of a sailor who left his wife in a little shop, and, after being shipwrecked in the tropics, returned after she had married another childhood friend, Tennyson seems deliberately to have applied a lavish, romantic style to the telling of a humble village tale. The basic story satisfied his friends who wanted him to write about contemporary English life; the romanticism pleased those who desired common life to appear in shining raiment; but a basket of fish [23] does not lose its identity by being called "Enoch's ocean-spoil in ocean-smelling osier."

Beside this ability to describe common life from the inside and to poke fun at high idealism through common sense, Tennyson clearly had a swashbuckling side which was vigorous enough for Fausset to call it "jingoistic." [24] One thinks immediately of national airs like "Britons, Guard Your Own," 1852, and "Riflemen, Form," 1859, and of the longer ballads and odes. "The Revenge," 1878, a ballad of Sir Richard Grenville's battle with the Spanish fleet off the Azores in 1591, and "The Defence of Lucknow," 1879, a ballad arising out of the Sepoy Rebellion in British India, are representatives of the longer patriotic poems. In them we find that strong reverence for the military and that respect for established authority that led Tennyson to support Governor Eyre of Jamaica when most of his liberal friends had joined a committee to force Eyre's recall and punishment. [25] The great "Ode on the Death of the Duke of Wellington," 1852 (considerably revised in 1853 and 1855) not only lauded the greatness of the soldier on the field of battle and in the slow and solemn funeral march the greatness of his memory, but suggested that the qualities of the soldier are also the most desirable qualities for the statesman. When the funeral march melts into the noise of battle and that is hushed by the cathedral choir, we are told that "on God and Godlike men we

---

[23] Walter Bagehot, "Wordsworth, Tennyson and Browning" (1864), *English Critical Essays: Nineteenth Century* (Oxford, 1945), p. 467.

[24] Hugh I'Anson Fausset, *Tennyson: A Modern Portrait* (London), Preface, 1929 edition.

[25] Tennyson (Hallam), *Memoir*, II, 40.

build our trust," with the clear implication that the Iron Duke was such a one (a passage reminiscent of Carlyle's hero-worship which finally found its focus on Sir Robert Walpole). The critical side of Tennyson's mind seems to have been turned toward domestic England, but to international England he gave only trust and adoration. His patriotism, anti-Gallicism, and admiration of the military point toward an "Ajax" robust masculinity.

The Ajax-Camilla strain is revealed within brief compass in the Prologue to *In Memoriam*, 1850. "Strong" is balanced by "love," "seen" by "embrace," "prove" by "believing." It is possible to go through the eleven quatrains of the Prologue and, listing the key words in two columns, to discover that there exists a very close balance between strong and soft words. This same romantic and antiromantic ambivalence which co-exists in *Enoch Arden* is apparent in two seemingly traditional poems. "Lilian," 1830, moves delicately from "Airy, fairy Lilian" in the first line to

> Like a rose-leaf I will crush thee,
>   Fairy Lilian. [IV, lines 4–5]

in the last two lines. Although the climax has been prepared for, its violence in a poem of this type is still jarring. In "'Come Not, When I am Dead,'" 1851, the familiar lament of the spurned lover imagining a repentant visit of the cruel one to his grave is full of deep bitterness mixed with world-weariness as the lover forbids his love to visit his grave, to "trample" around, to drop "foolish tears," and instructs her to "go by, go by," for he is "sick of time" and "desires to rest." Both poems should be considered deliberate attempts to mock the easy sentimentality of the traditional forms of love-lament.

When we consider the feminine-masculine *personae* of Tennyson's poems we find an equally notable ambivalence. The analysis of "The Palace of Art" (Chapter I) indicated that the soul of the poet is always referred to as "She." Despite the usual and incorrect assumption that all angels are feminine, it seems curious for a male poet to speak of his soul, or the soul of the artist *per se*, as being of the opposite gender. It is almost an anticipation of the Jungian theory that each person has an *anima* or anti-self which is opposite in sex and which influences the choice of person to whom the mature individual is sexually attracted.[26] In the discussion of *The Princess* there was observed the transvestism of women who behaved like men and men who dressed like women. When applied to the figure of the Prince, this ambivalence is notable not only in the matter of dress but also in the personality of a fighter who falls into a mystic trance in the midst of battle, a hero who rescues his beloved from drowning but is most attractive to the Princess when he is an invalid under her nursing care. The Princess herself is highly ambivalent, with traits of the male and the female, a scholar in study but easily made maternal by a little child, a fighter for principle who finds her complete self when she nurses her fiancé-foe back to health. Ida as nurse and mother does not invalidate the princess as intellectual, but provides the vital tension of the roles and relationships of women.

In Memoriam contains a considerable number of examples of bisexual masks for the poet to wear. In Chapter III there was some discussion of Tennyson's classical references to himself as half a person and the deceased as the other half. By extension of this basic image, he moves to the idea of the living "half" as the "widow" of the deceased. It was no doubt his four-fold use of the adjective "widow'd" to describe his bereaved state that so confused a contemporary journalist that he leaped to the conclusion that the great elegy had been written by a widow (page 84). In poem LII the writer counsels his heart to "fret not, like an idle girl," and in LX he likens his love for Arthur to that of

> some poor girl whose heart is set
> On one whose rank exceeds her own.
>
> [lines 3-4]

[26] John Killham, *Tennyson and "The Princess": Reflections of an Age* (London, 1958), p. 192 n; Buckley, *Tennyson*, p. 101.

In poem XCVII the poet observes a married couple and thinks of his own "spirit as of a wife."

In this rather strange willingness to think of himself as the female partner of a male friend, Tennyson was quite aware of the bisexuality involved and boldly described Hallam and Jesus Christ as male-female. Poem CIX describes Hallam as "manhood fused with female grace." In the *Memoir*, Tennyson defines Christ's pity as "the man-woman in Christ, the union of tenderness and strength." [27] The poet chose to wear so many masculine-feminine masks that there can be no question of Tennyson's belief in the bisexuality of a poet, of the best of men, and of the Divine Man.

In 1948, Lionel Stevenson found what he called the "high-born maiden symbol" in "The Lady of Shalott," "The Palace of Art," "Mariana," "Mariana in the South," "Lady Clare Vere de Vere," *Maud*, *The Princess*, "The Day Dream," and "Lancelot and Elaine." [28] He argued that the symbol represented the poet's own soul by way of a woman-figure. Referring to Professor W. D. Paden's work *Tennyson in Egypt*,[29] he reasoned that since no such theme can be found in the early poems studied there in terms of the psychological meanings of imagery, Tennyson must owe it to his later reading of Shelley, in particular to his "To a Skylark," "Epipsychidion," "The Witch of Atlas," and *Queen Mab*. As a poetic foreshadowing of later psychological theory, this must rank with the evolutionary theory included in *In Memoriam* nine years before the publication of *The Origin of Species*, and the pre-Freudian analyses of trauma and manic depression in *Maud*. It also takes its place as one more document in the file of the masculine-feminine *personae* of the poet. But the theme can be carried further than Stevenson has taken it. Let us assume that Mariana, the Lady,

[27] Tennyson (Hallam), *Memoir*, I, 326.
[28] Lionel Stevenson, "The 'High-Born Maiden' Symbol in Tennyson," *PMLA*, LXIII (March–June 1948), 234 ff.
[29] W. D. Paden, *Tennyson in Egypt: A Study of the Imagery in His Earlier Work* (Lawrence, Kansas, 1942).

the Soul, and Lady Clare are *animae* or female counterparts of the soul of the poet. Then the soul is represented as mourning, isolated from a life which would mean the death of the soul, luxuriating in a selfish aestheticism, and disdainful of love. But all of these poems have a more basic similarity than the theme of the high-born maiden—they are all poems of rejection. If there is a maiden there is also a male who either rejects (as in "The Lady of Shalott," "Mariana," "Mariana in the South," "Lancelot and Elaine"), or is rejected ("Lady Clare Vere de Vere," "Locksley Hall," *Maud, Enoch Arden*, "Edwin Morris," *Locksley Hall Sixty Years After*). According to this broader concept, the poet not only portrays female figures who are projections of his inner states, but he also makes a moral judgment upon them as worthy or unworthy of acceptance. Thus the ego becomes the censor of the *anima* as the poet rejects the soul of the Palace of Art, Letty Hill ("Edwin Morris"), and Lady Clare; weeps with Mariana, Oenone, and Elaine; and accepts Amy and the Princess after a period of adjustment. By this reading, the "high-born maiden theme" becomes a part of the total Tennysonian indecisiveness and tension between withdrawal and return, rejection and acceptance. It stresses both the femine *persona* of the poet and his masculine role of judgment and identification or refusal to identify.

Throughout this study the terms ambiguity, ambivalence, paradox and dubiety have been used without giving much attention either to specific definition or to comparison of meaning. Paden defined Tennyson's ambiguity as "one image suffused with two emotions." [30] Stange defined ambiguity as "the dialogue of the mind with itself . . . the anguished perception of the oppositions that rend the poet and his world." Personal ambivalence was "his tendency . . . to surround his personal subjects with the rich trappings of myth and legend," and social ambivalence the experience of the "nineteenth-

[30] *Ibid.*, p. 14.

century artist, rejected by the world, who at one moment rejoices in his isolation, and at another struggles to assert himself as *sacer vates*." [31] Cleanth Brooks, in his subtle analysis of "Tears, Idle Tears," states that the concluding lines of that poem express Tennyson's "paradox, ambiguity, and ironic contrast." [32]

These are significant and helpful definitions and identifications, and Tennyson scholarship is indebted to the fine studies from which they come. However, in line with the central thought of this study, it seems important first to point out the resemblances of these terms (ambiguity, ambivalence, paradox, dubiety) and then indicate their differences. For Tennyson, all these qualities were the product of tension. He was ambiguous because he was torn; he was ambivalent because he was divided; he was dubious because he was forced to put his trust in assurances of which he could not be sure; and he was never paradoxical, because paradox is a state of perfect balance in which each of the antitheses remains at an extreme and draws with strength and constancy approximately equal to its opposite. Agony, confusion, fear, and limited assertion are too characteristic of Tennyson's poetic statement to admit the likelihood of balanced tensions.

Having established the resemblances, let us explore the differences. Bush reminds us that "Tears Idle Tears" is "a series of inspired variations" on four lines from Virgil (*Aeneid*, I, line 462; IV, line 449; X, line 465, and *Georgics* IV, line 375), which include "*lacrimae inanes*" (or synonyms), and thus supply the title to Tennyson's poem, but also affirmed that it came "from the center of Tennyson's own soul." [33] Cleanth Brooks used it as a supreme example of Tennyson's ambiguity. Are

[31] G. Robert Stange, "Tennyson's Mythology—a Study of 'Demeter and Persephone,'" *English Literary History*, XXI (March 1954), 68.

[32] Cleanth Brooks, *The Well Wrought Urn: Studies in the Structure of Poetry* (New York, 1947), pp. 153 ff.

[33] Douglas Bush, *Mythology and the Romantic Tradition* (Cambridge, Mass., 1937), p. 228.

these tears "idle" or meaningful? He concludes that they spring from the deep, universal causation of a "divine despair" and from the poet's personal memory of "the days that are no more." "The dead past seems to the living man [Tennyson] as unfamiliar and fresh in its sadness as the living present seems to the dying man" [Hallam]. Then ambiguity arises out of a cluster of meanings which are subtly offered, and not for the choice of this or that nor for all, but for now this, now that, in an agony of debate.

R. F. Brissenden described Samuel Richardson as a man with "a divided heart . . . essentially ambivalent," with "no great understanding or control of the conflicting inner forces he was about to release." [34] Alfred Tennyson was essentially ambivalent in the sense that the divided heart always reduced any question to a socially acceptable *pro* and a personally tempting *con*. This procedure of noting both statement and denial has been not the imposition of a critical canon from the outside, but the exposition of an inner and continuing tendency. Brissenden's description of Richardson does not describe Tennyson so far as understanding is concerned, although Tennyson, even recognizing his ambivalence, was perhaps unable to control it to the point of omitting it entirely from his writing. It is Tennyson's wry comprehension of his own psychological mechanics that provides an added enrichment of his poetry.

Tennyson classified dogmatism as "the swift decision of one who sees only half the truth." [35] But if his double vision gave him both halves of the truth, it also left him with segments he could neither reconcile nor reassemble, so it was obvious that general dubiety would result. This must often have been the psychological formula. He recognized the socially acceptable statement of the truth, he responded deeply to his own poetic vision of an inner statement of the truth, and looking with dis-

[34] R. F. Brissenden, *Samuel Richardson* (London, 1958), pp. 18, 19, 20.
[35] Tennyson (Hallam), *Memoir*, I, 37.

may upon his vacillation between the two poles, he was left in
a condition of intellectual dubiety about each.

> O weary life! O weary death!
> O spirit and heart made desolate!
> O damned vacillating state!

["Supposed Confessions of a Second-Rate Sensitive Mind"
(1830), lines 188–190]

VI

Tendency versus Correction

In the vast welter of the *Biographia Literaria*, Samuel Taylor Coleridge insisted that Shakespeare, who was "no mere child of nature; no *automaton* of genius; no passive vehicle of inspiration, possessed by the spirit, not possessing it; first studied patiently, meditated deeply, understood minutely, till knowledge, become habitual and intuitive, wedded itself to his habitual feelings, and at length gave birth to that stupendous power, by which he stands alone, with no equal or second in his own class. . . ."[1]

Such a distinction between "possessing" inspiration and "being possessed by" inspiration arises out of a recognition of the varying degrees of self-awareness in men. As for the poet who recognizes neither the source nor the mechanics of his own behavior, the reader may, in some regards, understand him better than the poet understands himself. For example, when Baudelaire rejected the bourgeois ideal of marriage and the home,[2] he did so because he felt the intensity of a human relationship to be its supreme measure of value. From the bias of this quantitative sensationalism, he arrived at the ideal of a sexual relationship which does not issue in children and from which cruelty is not only inseparable but the final essential nuance.[3] Until Baudelaire had traveled this road far enough to begin hearing *les ailes de la démence*, he seemed unable or unwilling to recognize its certain destination.

[1] Samuel Taylor Coleridge, *Biographia Literaria* (London, 1949), p. 157.

[2] Charles Pierre Baudelaire, *Intimate Journals*, Preface by trans. Christopher Isherwood (Hollywood, 1947), p. 9.

[3] *Ibid.*, Introduction by W. H. Auden, p. 21.

By contrast with Baudelaire's unseeing velocity, the poetry of John Donne makes us immediately aware of the poet's exquisite self-consciousness, the quick glance of the inner eye that catches the devious motive before it slips behind the mask of self-esteem. In "A Hymn to God the Father" we glimpse the genuine desire to be forgiven, hand in hand with the honest admission that he still commits sin even while regretting it and asking forgiveness.

> Wilt thou forgive those sinnes, through which I runne,
>   And do run still: though still I do deplore?

In the "Holy Sonnets" we recognize this same quality of wry self-knowledge.

> I durst not view heaven yesterday; and to day
> In prayers, and flattering speaches I court God;
> Tomorrow I quake with true fears of his rod.
> So my devout fitts come and go away
> Like fantastique Ague: save that here
> Those are my best dayes, when I shake with fear.[4]

Many readers of the voluminous Tennyson have so disliked the dimity-daintiness of "O Darling Room" (to which Croker objected so violently), phrases like "neater and completer . . . nothing can be sweeter"[5] (to which anyone would object), or the accents of the schoolma'am that so annoyed Bulwer-Lytton in "The Miller's Daughter," that they have assumed that the poet was insensitive to the critical reactions of others, and quite unself-conscious. This chapter presents evidence of his awareness of himself, his correction of his own tendencies, and the biographical forces which influenced both self-criticism and self-correction.

There are many poems which reveal his extraordinary, even tortured self-awareness. His sardonic insight into the poseur concealed within many an aesthete was revealed in the juvenile

---

[4] John Donne, *The Divine Poems* edited and arranged by Helen Gardner. (Oxford, 1952), p. 16.

[5] *Maud*, XX, i, 806–807.

study of 1830, "A Character." He "spake of beauty" and lamented the dull creatures who found no "divinity in grass," "life in dead stones," or "spirit in air,"

> Then looking as 't were in a glass,
> He smooth'd his chin and sleek'd his hair,
> And said the earth was beautiful.
>
> [lines 10–12]

Consider the multifaceted awareness of the self involved in the title "The Supposed Confessions of a Second-Rate Sensitive Mind Not in Unity with Itself," 1850. Are these confessions real or "supposed"; is the mind called "second-rate" in honest humility or false modesty which awaits the kind assurance that the mind is really first-rate; is the mind sensitive in the perceptive sense or in the sense of being easily wounded; does "itself" refer to the author's mind, or is the poem an impersonal study; is its central figure a real or a supposed penitent? About the validity of the phrase "not in unity with itself" there can be no question. In this psyche-labyrinth of a poet-Minotaur, Theseus needs more than thread. We have already quoted the closing lines from the "Supposed Confessions" in which the poet expresses his weariness of being shaken by the twin fears of life and of death, and his sad knowledge that the spirit to believe and the heart to dare become barren in such a terrifying and "damned vacillating state!"

H. M. McLuhan pointed out that in "Locksley Hall," 1842, "as vision yields to vision, the speaker experiences a moment of ironic consciousness. And it is in the recognition of the timing and placing of such effects that much of the enjoyment of Tennyson consists." [6] A closer reading would reveal not less than three such moments of "ironic consciousness" when the mind turns upon the speaker and mocks his utterance. The young prophet without a beard had just melodramatically

[6] H. M. McLuhan, "Tennyson and the Romantic Epic," in John Killham (ed.), *Critical Essays on the Poetry of Tennyson* (London, 1960), p. 94.

cursed social wants, lies, forms and gold when something in the orotund echo of his voice makes him falter, "Well—'t is well that I should bluster!" (line 63). The bugle-horn of his comrades calls him and its brassy blast gives him the power to see himself as they would see him, "my foolish passion . . . a target for their scorn" and causes him to ask, "shall it not be scorn to me?" (line 146). From another of the interminable series of sulphurous visions he jerks back into shamed self-recognition with, "Fool, again the dream, the fancy! but I *know* my words are wild" (line 173).

And if the first "Locksley Hall" has three moments of ironic self-recognition, the second *Locksley Hall Sixty Years After*, 1886, has at least four. Grandfather, who is an insatiable monologuist, has just accused his grandson of "boyish babble" when he catches a glimpse of himself in the youth's eyes and mutters uneasily, "I myself have often babbled doubtless of a foolish past" (line 7). After waxing rhetorical about feeding "the budding rose of boyhood with the drainage of your sewer," and "maiden fancies wallowing in the troughs of Zolaism," the silence of the listener makes him supply a criticism which has not been made:

Heated am I? you—you wonder—well, it scarce becomes
    mine age—
Patience! let the dying actor mouth his last upon the stage.
        [lines 151–152]

Suddenly the speaker remembers that he is an old man speaking to a youth and begs, "Nay, your pardon, cry your 'Forward,' yours are hope and youth, but I—" (line 225). After noting the way beauty dwindles as science grows, and feeling sorry for "Poor old Heraldry, poor old History, poor old Poetry," the speaker wryly adds, "Poor old voice of eighty crying after voices that have fled!" (line 251). In all these moments the flashing gift of objectivity throws its light far down the corridors of the poet's personality and his understanding of himself.

In Poem XVI of *In Memoriam*, 1850, the mourning poet was troubled by the subtle changes in his grief and the evidence these changes gave of inner dividedness.

> What words are these have fallen from me?
> Can calm despair and wild unrest
> Be tenants of a single breast,
> Or sorrow such a changeling be?

In Poem XXIV, Tennyson suddenly and unexpectedly steps apart from his sorrow, surveys both his past memories and his present grief and asks himself with wry honesty if he really had such a good time when his friend was alive.

> And was the day of my delight
> As pure and perfect as I say?

Four lines from "Will," written in 1856, reveal a strong kinship with Donne in their play upon appearance, reality, and psychological compulsion as the poet discusses a fault which he now recognizes as "venial," but which once seemed to be "genial," and which, even while he recognizes it, is "recurring and suggesting still!" In so involved an analysis of personality, past and present, it is no wonder that his "footsteps halt" as if he had been "toiling in immeasurable sand."

In "The Passing of Arthur," 1869, the king is in a funeral barge on a dark lake. He refers to the way he must go and to those who will be his companions; then with an utterly characteristic break, he turns from the listening Bedivere and peers inside himself to see if he really believes what he has just said:

> I am going a long way
> With these thou seest—if indeed I go—
> For all my mind is clouded with a doubt—
> To the island-valley of Avilion [lines 256–259]

In the "Supposed Confessions" the poet recognizes that the essential duality of his personality makes the unified vision impossible; in "Locksley Hall" the speaker indicts himself as a blusterer, the victim of a foolish passion he ought to have scorned, and a foolish dreamer whose words are wild; in the second

Locksley Hall the grandfather confesses that he babbles, that he is more heated than is dignified in an old man, and that his vision has become the victim of his age; in *In Memoriam* the poet questions his tendency to enhance the past through the transforming power of memory and is troubled by the emotional evidences of his divided will; in "Will" he admits that his double vision does not clarify the issue and may leave him unable to act; in "The Passing of Arthur" his doubt makes him question his own identity, his personal destiny, and his ultimate destination. These moments of wry awareness, of the balancing of spiritual accounts, are the reward of the perceptive reader. They pierce through the mask of anonymity the poet wears and confront him and his reader with the moment of truth.

The poet who is so aware of himself is quite capable of correcting his own poetic tendencies. When Tennyson wrote "The Palace of Art," 1832, he could with integrity and whole-heartedness give his imagination free rein in building and furnishing that palace with the great cultural treasury of the western world. But with critical awareness of his own recessive tendencies, he knew that even the creative artist has no right to dwell solitarily in the midst of lavish beauty while men starve and infants are slain by their "Mamonite mothers." [7] "He would have been glad . . . to persuade himself that pure non-instrumental loveliness was socially beneficent, and that the artist can best serve his fellows by giving them shapes of beauty, imaginative creations unsullied by vulgar preachment. And yet the distinction between social-minded and wickedly irresponsible aestheticism was difficult to maintain." [8] Buckley pointed out that for Tennyson the opposite distinction was just as difficult to maintain. "To illustrate his own belief that 'the Godlike life is with man and for man,' he wrote 'The Palace of Art,' an allegory of the aesthetic soul that vainly shrinks from the encroachment of 'uncertain shapes,' the lengthening

[7] *Maud*, I, line 45.

[8] Hoxie Neale Fairchild, *Religious Trehds in English Poetry: 1830–1880* (New York, 1957), IV, 104.

shadows of a dark reality. Yet he was in truth still too pre-occupied with the studied depiction of dreamful ease to vitalize the artist's conflict; the lush *décor* of the pleasure dome remained more vivid to him than the homely 'cottage in the vale' where the converted soul was to learn the alchemy of love." [9]

In *The Princess*, 1847, Tennyson is the foe of those forces of contemporary life which separated man and woman, woman and child, college training and family life, the heart and the mind. Indeed he insists, in prophetically modern terms, that the essential nature of the individual can be known only in relationship, not in isolation. Tennyson never falters from recognizing marriage, home, and child as the central relationships of this life. Thus the intense and lethal debate of "The Two Voices," 1834, finds its release in the symbolism of a Christian family, and the wild and wandering cries of *In Memoriam* are finally blended into the wedding hymn at its close.

Roy P. Basler, in an article entitled "Tennyson the Psychologist," points out the extraordinarily subtle psychological insights to be found in the poet's monodrama *Maud*, 1856.

Even under fortuitous circumstances the hero might have experienced difficulty in making an adjustment to the "cruel madness of love," for his is essentially an introvertish ego. His dominant wish is to hide, to bury himself in himself. From the time of his father's death his life has been isolated by wish as well as by circumstance, and he resents the return of Maud's family to the neighboring Hall because of an unconscious fear of Maud herself as a source of danger to all that is his. This dominant wish to hide . . . is the essential obsession which throughout the poem marks his reaction to fear and pain, and culminates in Part II in dementia, the diagnostic of which is that he is dead and buried. This introversion is at the root of his attempt to adopt the cynical pose in which he will observe human affairs but not participate in them.

[9] Jerome Hamilton Buckley, *The Victorian Temper: A Study in Literary Culture* (Cambridge, Mass., 1951), p. 73.

The plot of the poem, however, is not based primarily upon the conventional love theme, as has often been supposed, but rather upon the theme of psychic conflict between the phases of the hero's personality. This view is substantiated by Tennyson's own statement that the poem is a drama of the soul in which "different phases of passion in one person take the place of different characters." [10]

Applying these insights to the poem, the following pattern emerges. The male protagonist at first desires to bury himself in self and the past. Maud draws him out of the self through love. But as was the case with his love for his father (and in a lesser degree with his love for his mother), his love for Maud ends in bloodshed, death and separation. His past has captured the present. Then the hero buries himself psychologically in madness, actually feeling dead and buried and resenting the shallowness of his grave. Once again he emerges, this time into war. His involvement in war stems from love of country and a desire to identify himself with the lives of other men. But war, made attractive to him by his capacity to love, involves necessary bloodshed and may issue in death and ultimate separation. So the pattern remains the same: emergence in love of father-mother-Maud-country, all ending in bloodshed, death and separation.

It is naïve to assume that the poet understood nothing of the underlying conflict of his own monodrama. As Mr. Basler says, "the amazing thing about *Maud* . . . is . . . that it antedates by half a century the writings of Sigmund Freud." [11] Tennyson is so aware of his own tendency to retreat that he can portray a hero emerging again and again, only to face the same tragic combination upon each emergence, and even in his madness imagining himself a snail which ventured forth into a "dim water-world" and died:

[10] Roy P. Basler, "Tennyson the Psychologist," *South Atlantic Quarterly*, XLIII (April 1944), 147–148.

[11] *Ibid.*, p. 143.

Always I long to creep
Into some still cavern deep,
There to weep, and weep, and weep
My whole soul out to thee.
                    [Part II, lines 235–238]

The movement of meaning in *In Memoriam* is neither the achievement of a settled faith with which many of Tennyson's contemporaries credited it, nor is it the "determined social dedication" of Buckley's thesis.[12] But there are elements of self-correction as Tennyson first apologizes to his favorite brother Charles for having written that Arthur Hallam meant more to him than his own brothers, and as he explains to Edmund Lushington that although he desires new, living friends, he can never again give his whole heart as he had given it to Hallam. Then in the Epilogue, there is a kind of self-correction in Tennyson's odd blend of biology and pantheism. Hallam was a "type" of a higher race of men that was to come; Edmund and Cecilia's son will somehow "type" Hallam's superior qualities in himself and so pass them on to human progress; and Hallam will henceforth be neither in the Heaven of the Christian faith nor in all men, but by a kind of spiritual atomism, by his death mingle with the universe.

The cryptic "Merlin and the Gleam," 1889, is open to many varied methods of interpretation, but there can be no argument about the transition from a retreat to "desolate hollows" in Stanza IV to the return to healing scenes of "lowly labor" in Stanza V, representing a self-corrective movement from artistic isolation to social participation. In the "Marriage of Geraint" it is pointed out that even marriage can become a kind of isolation, and Enid sorrows over the love-retirement of her own husband, fearing that men will see in his devotion to his wife an "uxoriousness" bordering on "effeminacy" (here used as a synonym for social ineffectiveness). The youthful "Tithonus" seemed "to his great heart none other than a god" when he

12 Buckley, *The Victorian Temper*, p. 87.

received the gift of immortality from Aurora. But the aged Tithonus begged querulously to rejoin ordinary humanity, to know healing, restful death, and in no way "to vary from the kindly race of men." This same longing to be identified with mankind and to participate in the common lot, even if it means death, may also be found in the last lines of *Maud*—

It is better to fight for the good than to rail at the ill;
I have felt with my native land, I am one with my kind,
I embrace the purpose of God, and the doom assign'd.

—a passage pregnant with special Tennyson meanings: the deed more creative than the word, the longing to be lost in corporate humanity, the desire to find God's purpose in the world, and the conviction that even embracing the purpose of God does not exempt a man from the assigned doom of death.

The poet's critique of the goal of beauty was explicit and clear in "The Palace of Art" (Chapter I). The examination and rejection of an isolating holiness was implicit in "The Holy Grail" (Chapter II). When we are aware of this constant dialogue of statement and correction we cannot but conjecture concerning its sources. It has already been pointed out that the basic source is the poet's own divided soul—ambiguous, ambivalent, and dubious. The third division of this chapter examines some of the biographical forces which operated for and against the Tennysonian tendency to retreat from the world and to return to it again.

Tennyson faces us with the problem of a poet who presents a view of life—and then proceeds to argue against his own presentation, by word, by tone, by choice of topic, or through the concealing play of masks. This continuous poetic debate is so characteristic that J. H. Buckley, in *The Victorian Temper*, used the title of an early poem, "The Two Voices," as the title of his chapter on Tennyson, just as the title of this study is borrowed from that poem. Let us examine some of the influences which produced this almost Hegelian dialectic in verse.

Tennyson was a child of his age and nation, and the British genius for steering a middle course between quite irreconcilable opposites is nowhere clearer than in his literary documents. For example, in dealing with the Arthurian legend, he set up two symbols of decay and dissolution: first, the adulterous and passionate extramarital love of Lancelot and Guinevere, which represented the kind of sexual excess abhorrent to Tennyson and to his age; second, the Holy Grail, which represented an excessive religious fanaticism which makes a man inoperative and useless for the causes of this life. Tennyson evidently preferred that middle ground on which a man loves a woman just passionately enough to want to marry her, and having taken her to keep her, and keeping her to remain true to his vows, "forsaking all others." This was the kind of Tennysonian solution that led Sir Harold Nicolson to say that he approved "neither of voluptuousness nor of asceticism," but believed that the necessities of biology should be so mingled with civic virtue as to produce that pillar of the social order, the English home. [13] Thus the middle course between sexual freedom and other-worldly self-denial that the English-speaking world chose was the very course the poet steered.

Besides being a peculiarly British and Victorian poet, Tennyson was also an heir to that high birthright of the poet-bard-prophet so powerfully presented by Percy Bysshe Shelley in his *Defence of Poetry*:

But poets, or those who imagine and express this indestructible order, are not only the authors of language and of music, of the dance, and architecture, and statuary and painting: they are the inventors of the arts of life, and the teachers who draw into a certain propinquity with the beautiful and the true, that partial apprehension of the agencies of the invisible world which is called religion. . . . Poets, according to the circumstances of the age and nation in which they appeared, were called, in the earlier epochs of the world, legislators or

[13] Sir Harold Nicolson, *Tennyson: Aspects of His Life, Character and Poetry* (Boston and New York, 1922), p. 244.

prophets; a poet essentially comprises and unites both these characters. For he not only beholds intensely the present as it is, and discovers those laws according to which present things ought to be ordered, but he beholds the future in the present, and his thoughts are the germs of the flower and the fruit of latest time.[14]

Thus there was for Tennyson, or any other nineteenth-century poet, a tradition of the role of the poet not only in art but also in ethics, religion, law, politics, education and international affairs. There is every evidence that Tennyson took his poetic task with the greatest seriousness, and he must have felt considerable pressure upon him from the past to perform that prophetic function in an age when he was the bridge between poets who died young and the new schools which arose after his own artistic career was well on its way.

In the Cambridge edition of Tennyson's poetic and dramatic works, there is a note that line two hundred and twenty-two of "The Palace of Art" was derived from Arthur Hallam's essay "Theodicaea Novissima."[15] The note itself is of no particular importance here, but it points to another influence upon the poet's conception of his role and function in his own age. Tennyson was influenced in choice of topic and manner of treatment by his friends, and most strongly by those friendships that reached back to Cambridge school days and the "Cambridge Conversazione Society." Fausset somewhat imaginatively pictures the poet when "he felt sated even by his own seductive music . . . then the spirit of the Apostles rose up in judgment against him. Here were men braving the mystery of life, while he played with its echoes . . . he would turn with angry effort and seek to acquit himself by more manly, serious verse."[16] Nicolson puts the matter rather more soberly and

[14] Percy Bysshe Shelley, *Literary and Philosophical Criticism* (London, 1909), p. 124.

[15] W. J. Rolfe (ed.), *The Poetic and Dramatic Works of Alfred, Lord Tennyson* (Boston, 1898), p. 804.

[16] Hugh I'Anson Fausset, *Tennyson: A Modern Portrait*, Traveller's Library (London, 1929), p. 31.

objectively by pointing out that the influence of the "Apostles" was very strong on "the moral and social significance of poetry." [17] They were idealistic young men of college age who had an overly serious view of their own importance in the scheme of things and who believed ardently, like thousands then and later, that they should devote their lives to making the world a better place in which to live. Friends who were in the Apostles, or fellow undergraduates, continued to have a strong influence in this direction as long as they and the poet lived. R. C. Trench, later Anglican Archbishop of Dublin, said to his poet friend, when they were at Trinity College, "Tennyson, we cannot live in art." [18] This was the same Trench who was quoted by Hallam in a letter to W. B. Donne, January 29, 1831: "Trench considers a man who reads Cicero or Bacon nowadays, much as he would a man who goes asleep on the edge of a mad torrent, and dreams of a garden of cucumbers." [19] Many years later the octogenarian poet was to echo his school friend's dictum in the poem "Romney's Remorse," 1889. The artist, being asked by God why he deserted his wife and children, replies, "Nay Lord, for *Art*," and then bitterly reflects that he has lost "salvation for a sketch" (lines 132, 140).

James Spedding, after reading "The Palace of Art," "St. Simeon Stylites," "The Two Voices," and "The Vision of Sin" commented not only that they represented "work at the highest level" but more significantly that from them we may gather "his moral theory of life and its issues and of that which constitutes a sound condition of the soul." [20] Such a commendation sounds rather more like a description of the excellences of a sermon than of four poems. But this kind of didactic expectation pressed in upon the poet, vitally shaping his conception of his poetic task.

[17] Nicolson, *Tennyson, Aspects*, p. 83.

[18] Hallam, Lord Tennyson, *Alfred, Lord Tennyson: A Memoir by His Son* (New York, 1897), I, 118.

[19] John Killham, *Tennyson and "The Princess": Reflections of an Age* (London, 1958), p. 26.

[20] Tennyson (Hallam), *Memoir*, I, 192.

In his biography of Edward FitzGerald, A. McKinley Terhune points out that that friend and contemporary writer believed "Tennyson had missed his objective as England's poet. In 1851, when lamenting, as he frequently did, the general decay into which he believed the country had fallen, he exclaimed, 'If one could save the Race, what a Cause it would be: not for one's own glory as a member of it, nor even for its glory as a Nation: but because it is the only spot in Europe where Freedom keeps her place. Had I Alfred's voice, I would not have mumbled for years over *In Memoriam* and *The Princess*, but sung such strains as would have revived the Μαραθωνομακονς ἄνδρας to guard the territory they had won.'" [21]

Tiresias and Other Poems, published in 1885, contained an introductory poem, "To E. FitzGerald," in which the poet said he was "nearing seventy-four" and his friend had "touch'd at seventy-five." The title poem, written much earlier than the publication date would indicate, contains the line: "virtue must express itself in deed" (line 85). It is almost as if the aged poet were replying to "Fitz's" criticism and giving the same hearty agreement in age as in youth with its basic conviction.

As we might expect, Arthur Henry Hallam too was a powerful influence toward the assumption of a prophetic role. The poet's grandson, Charles Tennyson, relates that under the influence of Arthur and the Cambridge circle, Alfred Tennyson began to feel that excessive absorption in the pursuit of abstract beauty was one of his particular and dangerous temptations. The poet recognized that it was "easy for him to withdraw into himself and to pursue in isolation his own fancies and speculations, avoiding those human contacts which he often found so distressing. . . . a poet's work . . . must be related to the great problems and passions of mankind. The advice of friends like Venables, who urged a greater concentration on the

---

[21] A. McKinley Terhune, *Life of Edward FitzGerald* (New Haven, 1947), pp. 127–128. Μαραθωνομακονς ἄνδρας—"men who fought at Marathon."

broad and common interests of the time and of universal humanity, strengthened this tendency." [22]

In his review of Tennyson's 1830 volume, Arthur Hallam had leaned in the direction of pure aestheticism: "It is not true, as the exclusive admirers of Mr. Wordsworth would have it, that the highest species of poetry is the reflective; it is a gross fallacy, that because certain opinions are acute or profound, the expression of them by the imagination must be eminently beautiful. Whenever the mind of the artist suffers itself to be occupied, during its periods of creation, by any other predominant motive than the desire of beauty, the result is false in art." [23] This was a position he was later to repudiate in further correspondence with the poet. Tennyson had earlier recognized and expressed in correspondence the concern lest he and the other Apostles "lose sight of the real in seeking the ideal." [24]

It is said that Thomas Woolner suggested to Tennyson the themes for *Enoch Arden* and "Aylmer's Field" because he felt poets should write more frequently about the common life of men in their own generation. [25] John Ruskin quite agreed and in a letter to Tennyson about the *Idylls of the King* recommended his and Woolner's point of view with characteristic eloquence and earnestness:

Treasures of wisdom there are in it, and word-painting such as never was yet for concentration, nevertheless it seems to me that so great power ought not to be spent on visions of things past but on the living present. For one hearer capable of feeling the depth of this poem I believe ten would feel a depth quite as great if the stream flowed through things nearer the hearer. . . . I cannot but think that the intense masterful and unerring transcript of an actuality, and the relation of a story of any real human life as a poet would watch and analyze it, would

---

[22] Charles B. L. Tennyson, *Alfred Tennyson* (New York, 1949), p. 131.

[23] T. H. Vail Motter (ed.), *The Writings of Arthur Hallam* (New York, 1943), p. 184.

[24] Tennyson (Hallam), *Memoir*, I, 71.   [25] *Ibid.*, II, 7.

make all men feel more or less what poetry was, as they felt what Life and Fate were in their instant workings.

This seems to me the true task of the modern poet. And I think I have seen faces, and heard voices by road and street side, which claimed or conferred as much as ever the loveliest or saddest of Camelot. As I watch them, the feeling continually weighs upon me, day by day, more and more, that not the grief of the world but the loss of it is the wonder of it. I see creatures so full of all power and beauty, with none to understand or teach or save them. The making in them of miracles and all cast away, for ever lost as far as we can trace. And no "in memoriam." [26]

In 1889, in "Romney's Remorse," Tennyson expressed his continued agreement with Ruskin's and Woolner's criticisms through the lips of the painter, Romney:

> I have stumbled back again
> Into the common day, the sounder self.
>
> [lines 32-33]

Not only did personal friends instruct the poet concerning the nature of his poetic task; journalists and editors added their pleas. In *Hogg's Weekly Instructor* for December 25, 1847, the editor asked, "Why does not Alfred Tennyson leave the Midian of his retirement to point the people's way to the coming Canaan?" Aubrey de Vere, in a composite review of Tennyson's *Poems*, 1842, and *The Princess*; *The Poetical Works of Shelley*; and Richard Monckton Milnes' *Life, Letters and Literary Remains of John Keats* said that the writings of Keats and Shelley had the defect "of appearing poetry distilled from poetry rather than drawn from the living sources of life and truth," whereas Tennyson's verse seemed to have moved deliberately and praiseworthily away from an "ideal" art of fanciful invention, toward a "national" art focused upon immediate actualities. [27] *The Christian Examiner* had urged Tennyson before the two

---

[26] *Ibid.*, I, 453-454.

[27] Aubrey de Vere, "Review of Shelley, Milnes [Keats], and Tennyson," *Edinburgh Review*, XC (October, 1849), 432.

volumes of 1842 to "fulfill a poet's mission to his age, inspired and inspiring" and to "enter the sphere of active interests, the momentous struggles of great principles." [28] Similar advice was offered by the *Westminster Review*, Christopher North in *Blackwood's Magazine*, the *Monthly Repository and Review*, and John Stuart Mill in the *London Review*.[29]

More examples could easily be collected. But perhaps these are enough to indicate that not only were the Victorian conscience and the high Shelleyan doctrine of legislator-prophet-priest shaping the poet, but also the influence of his friends and contemporaries was strongly in the direction of drawing Tennyson out of the past, out of his solitary moods, out of his Keatsian lusciousness into a harsher world of contested values and compromised actions. So effective was this influence that when Tennyson died, Thomas Henry Huxley seemed unable to decide whether he was rhyming the decease of a poet or a politician:

> And lay him gently down among
> The men of state, the men of song:
> The men who would not suffer wrong;
> The thought-worn chieftains of the mind,
> Head servants of the human kind.[30]

Without question the "publicity agent" of the new science would have applauded any decision that led a poet away from dreams and the past back to modern life and the indigestible but thrilling discoveries of modern science.

But by one of the strangest ironies of human interaction, these very friends who sought to draw Tennyson out of retreat also operated powerfully toward retreat—indeed, they were a retreat. At first there was the tight little literary circle of the Somersby parsonage crowded with dark, foreign-looking

[28] C. C. Felton, *The Christian Examiner*, XXXIII, 305.

[29] Joyce Green, "Tennyson's Development During the 'Ten Years' Silence' (1832–1842)," *PMLA* (1951), p. 683.

[30] Thomas Henry Huxley, "Tennyson" (poem), *Nineteenth Century* XXXII (November 1892), 831.

Tennysons; then there was the mutual admiration society of the "Apostles" and the continuation of this bulwark of confidence as long as these friends lived; and finally there was the warmth of secure admiration in his own home with his wife and family. Mildred Bozman, in her excellent introduction to the Everyman's Library Edition of Tennyson's poems, says that the fault in Tennyson's preparation for poetry may be found in his too prolonged, too sheltered confinement within the bounds of a loving family."[31] Sir Harold Nicolson suggests that between the years 1840–1892, Tennyson's greatest need was "to be contradicted."[32] The always frank FitzGerald wrote that Mrs. Tennyson "is a graceful lady, but I think she and other aesthetic and hysterical Ladies have hurt A. T., who, *quoad* Artist, would have done better to remain single in Lincolnshire, or married a jolly woman who would have laughed and cried without any reason why. But this is foolish and wicked Talking."[33] Although Hugh Fausset habitually overstates his case, he also recognized Tennyson's tendency to "hide in the retreat of a sensitive, pleasure-seeking temperament, barricaded from rude gusts by adoring friends, nor ever exposed to realities of poverty and neglect."[34]

There is another ironical twist of human interaction to be found in the life and reputation of Alfred Tennyson. Just as the very friends who tried to draw the poet out of retreat were themselves a retreat, so the very thing they wanted him to do is the thing he is today most criticized for doing. Rebuked in his own day for reluctance to play the prophetic role his contemporaries designed for him, he is criticized by modern critics for having attempted to play a prophetic role for which he was not qualified. Thus Sir Harold Nicolson writes about a

[31] Mildred Bozman, introduction, *Poems of Alfred Tennyson* (New York, 1949), p. xv.

[32] Nicolson, *Tennyson, Aspects*, p. 25.

[33] Edward FitzGerald, *Letters and Literary Remains* (London and New York, 1902–3), II, 189–190.

[34] Fausset, *Tennyson*, p. 37.

"great lyric poet" who was "tamed, controlled, labelled, and given a function unnatural to his genius," [35] and F. L. Lucas uses the figure of a "prophet's mantle" which was thrust upon him as he grew prominent, and which, at times at least, smothered his song. [36] Marjorie H. Nicolson pointed out his growing reputation as artist-craftsman and his declining reputation as prophet:

> It is the perfection of his artistry which is, for our age even more than for his own, the enduring grandeur of Tennyson. No modern poet has labored more truly on his work or believed more sincerely in the greatness of his art or has striven more nobly for perfection than did Tennyson. The writing of poetry was to him not a mere exercise, nor, on the other hand, the result of a fine fervor; it was a vocation in which he toiled as laboriously as any worker in metals or precious gems. The whirligig of time has brought in its revenges so far as his position as the voice of the English people is concerned; but if we have lost the old worship of the prophet, we have gained a new understanding and admiration of the artist. "The labor of the file" was Tennyson's labor. [37]

But let the modern critics be warned that when they compliment the qualities his contemporaries regretted and criticize the qualities they urged, they too are astride the "whirligig of time."

There is another influence toward retreat which the historian of literature might easily miss. After having referred to his literary ancestry, the sense in which he simply echoes the shibboleths of his age, and the influence of family and friends, there is still the individual personality with which to cope. Perhaps it was from his unhappy father who was a rejected first son that he received the dark bequest of wondering before the mysterious face of the unknowables, of ceaseless moral

---

[35] Nicolson, *Tennyson: Aspects*, p. 25.

[36] Frank Laurence Lucas, *Tennyson* (New York, 1957), p. 9.

[37] Marjorie H. Nicolson, introduction, *Selected Poems of Alfred Tennyson* (Boston, 1924), pp. 20–21.

questionings, of that flinging of an endless *Why* in the face of Providence which troubled his youthful and eager sense of the beauty of the world. Surely it was from him that he inherited those moods of darkness that descended upon him from time to time, shutting out all the light of nature, the life of the heart and the joy of the world, leaving only morbid sensitivity and a terribly heightened capacity for agony and doubt. At such times he seemed unable to see buds bursting to flower and flowers bringing forth the ripening fruit. He could only hear the dripping of dank decay, smell the rotting universe and feel the fretful, sharp-headed worm.

The pressure at Somersby was too high. The Doctor's [Alfred's father] health, both of body and mind, was seriously affected, and unhappily he began before long to turn to drink for consolation and relief . . . the Rector's distressing condition intensified his moods of depression and produced periods of extreme lethargy, so that he would lie in bed for forty-eight hours on end . . . the drink habit began to induce paroxysms of violence which were to have a disastrous effect on the family life . . .

   This exaggerated in him [Alfred] the family tendency towards melancholy and depression, the "black-bloodedness" of the Tennysons which was to afflict him all through life. The boyish self-confidence disappeared and he became subject to those moods of self-torment and remorse which are not uncommon in boys of sensitive nature, and which in him were intensified by the misery of his home life and the position of divided loyalty into which he often found himself forced between his father and his mother.[38]

Whatever the balance of heredity, environment, the mood of his age and the counsel of his friends, it is clear that Alfred Tennyson himself had that kind of nature and disposition which is inclined toward melancholy. One of the remarkable things about *In Memoriam* is the extraordinary persistence of the varied moods of sorrow, despair, and darkness for the seventeen-year period of writing, rewriting and arrangement. This

[38] Tennyson (Charles), *Tennyson*, pp. 46 ff.

was not simply the exploitation of an emotional experience to make writer's copy, but an experience which came to a poet so constituted by nature and background that for days and years the sense of loss persisted with the power and intensity that make artistic creation possible.

Out of this mixed inheritance, environment and individuality the mixed quality of criticism of his life and works arises. Critics past and present tend to see different Tennysons: the nature poet with meticulous power of observation; the poet of faith and religion; the poet of doubt and the progress of science; the Classical poet with great power to evoke the living moment out of the legendary past; the poet of sentimental portraiture—fair ladies for albums, the scenes of rural life and manners; the patriotic poet of the ballads, odes, and songs; the poet of self-conscious didacticism, the senior patriarch and prophet of England; the introspective poet of psychological fascination; the poet of decay and dissolution—"the mourning muse." There is a quite natural tendency, faced with this multifaceted personality and repertoire, to assume incorrectly that one of these roles is the natural function of Tennyson the man, and all the others are *personae* adopted by the poet for protection or forced upon him by his times.

VII

The Fragment versus the Whole

Earlier in this study, attempting to place Tennyson within the stream of classical western philosophy, his position was located between Pyrrhonism and Fideism as a doubter who longed for faith and the embracer of a faith which he could not quite trust. In this chapter, his position is classified from the point of view of the literary historian, and that position is related to the central thesis of this work as well as to modern life and letters.

The boy of fourteen who in 1824 mournfully carved on a rough stone the epitaph "Byron is dead," [1] was closely linked with those Romantic poets who were born into the alien climate of the eighteenth century. Just as for them, nature to him was alive with meaning and mood, the past was as living as the present, the realm of ideals was gripped in a titanic struggle with the forces of materialism, and the poet was an exile in his own time and his own country.

Not only chronologically but also as a poet-teacher in his youth and a poet-prophet in his maturity, he was a part of the Victorian Age which insisted that even the arts appear before the judgment bar of morality. There can be no question of his relevance to that age and of his importance in it, if these are based at all on the criteria of recognition, popularity, and reward. During his undergraduate days at Cambridge, on June 6, 1829, he won the Chancellor's Prize for his poem in blank verse, "Timbuctoo," a reworking of an earlier juvenile poem, "The Battle of Armageddon." [2] In September of the same

[1] Hallam, Lord Tennyson, *Alfred, Lord Tennyson: A Memoir by His Son* (New York, 1897), I, 4.
[2] *Ibid.*, p. 45.

year, Arthur Hallam wrote a letter to Gladstone, in which he said of his friend, "I consider Tennyson as promising fair to be the greatest poet of our generation, perhaps of our century." [3] While still a student at the university, Tennyson published *Poems, Chiefly Lyrical*, 1830. In spite of reviews of that volume and of *Poems, 1833*, which judicially mingled praise and censure, the Cambridge Union Society held a debate on the subject: "Tennyson or Milton—which is the greater poet?" [4] and the Apostles drank Alfred's health at their dinners with resounding cheers. Well might Colonel Newcome, just home from India, be perplexed by the literary taste of the younger generation. "He heard opinions that amazed and bewildered him: he heard that Byron was no great poet though a very clever man; he heard that there had been a wicked persecution against Mr. Pope's memory and fame, and that it was time to reinstate him; that his favourite Dr. Johnson talked admirable, but did not write English; that young Keats was a genius to be estimated in future days with young Raphael, and that a young gentleman of Cambridge, who had lately published two volumes of verses, might take rank with the greatest poets of all." [5]

By the publication of the two volumes of 1842, Tennyson was, for a large share of the reading public, the real Poet Laureate of Victorian England, one year before he was considered for that honor upon the death of Southey and eight years before he succeeded Wordsworth, who in 1845 had called him "the first of our living poets." [6] Until his death a full half century later, "he retained his place as oracle, as prophetic interpreter of the ideals, the tastes and prejudices of a troubled and tumultuous age." [7] In 1850, his *annus mirabilis*, the English

[3] *Ibid.*, p. 46.

[4] Charles B. L. Tennyson, *Alfred Tennyson* (New York, 1949), p. 141.

[5] William Makepeace Thackeray, *The Works of William Makepeace Thackeray VI: The Newcomes* (London, 1907), p. 209.

[6] Tennyson (Hallam), *Memoir*, I, 210.

[7] Jerome Hamilton Buckley, *The Victorian Temper: A Study in Literary Culture* (Cambridge, Mass., 1951), p. 66.

public read *In Memoriam* with awed enthusiasm; he became Poet Laureate of England, and married the sweetheart of eleven years, Emily Sellwood. In the years that followed, he was occasionally summoned to the palace by the Queen to read her his poems and to chat. Later he corresponded with Victoria, who in 1884 elevated him to the peerage.

But it would be a mistake to assume that his work received only adulation, although he had as much of that cloying diet as any poet in modern times. For example, when the poet followed the great success of *In Memoriam* with *Maud*, the reviewers were baffled by the change in content, style, and manner, and were moved to the slander of suggesting that either the "a" or the "u" might be omitted from the latter title with equal relevance.[8] The "very public voice"[9] of the poet so often displayed the widest variety in style and content that it would seem a logical assumption that his large audience may have been made up of a number of smaller particular audiences which responded to particular parts of his work. It may well be that many of the persons who loved the elegy hated the monodrama, and many who enjoyed the portraits of fair ladies may have cared for neither, and perhaps there were those who enjoyed "Mariana" and "The Lady of Shalott" and liked only the lyrics in *Maud*.

A varied poetry with particularity of audience may be a partial explanation for the difficulty of getting the Laureate's dramas produced. In 1879, *Becket* was ready for publication and, presumably, production. Fourteen years later, in 1893, it was finally produced, after many persuasions, by Henry Irving in New York City, where it became the most triumphant success of his whole American tour. Evidently a public which liked some of Tennyson did not necessarily assume that it would like everything of Tennyson. The "Ode on the Death of the Duke of Wellington" has been greatly admired by modern critics,

[8] Tennyson (Hallam), *Memoir*, I, 400.
[9] Hugh I'Anson Fausset, *Tennyson: A Modern Portrait* (London, 1923), p. iii.

yet it received a very cool and critical response when first published. Carlyle had praised Wellington as "the only Englishman in the Aristocracy who will have nothing to do with any manner of lie," [10] but of the ode he was content to mutter, "Tennyson's verses are naught. Silence alone is respectable on such an occasion." [11] The "Ode for the International Exhibition," 1862, was bitterly criticized for regretting the mixture of "works of peace with works of war," and for the intimation that the day of world peace was still "far away." Mixed reactions of this sort, in the light of his great public reputation, tend to indicate the existence of a divided response to a divided poet, as well as to remind us that the bard of Victorian England was often critical of what his contemporaries called progress. Despite the prevalence of "the Tennyson legend" and the poet's enormous personal popularity and influence, it must be realized that as his style of poetry changed along with the changes of his own mind and interests, his audience also shifted with the changing critical reaction.

The poet who was influenced by Wordsworth, Byron, Scott, Browning, Keats, Dobell, and Smith, at various times in his career, seemed also to have shared some of the ideals of the Pre-Raphaelite Brotherhood, although certainly not those which R. W. Buchanan castigated in "The Fleshly School of Poetry." [12] Although he eschewed the new hedonism of Fitz-Gerald's *Rubaiyat* and resisted the new Epicureanism of Walter Pater's *Renaissance*, [13] he shared with the P.R.B. their scrupulous delineation of detail, their wealth of symbolic image, and the strange hieratic flatness of the figures they grouped in their decorative panels.

[10] D. A. Wilson, *Carlyle* (New York, 1923–1934), III, 399.

[11] Charles Richard Sanders, "Carlyle and Tennyson," *PMLA*, LXXVI (March 1961), 90.

[12] R. W. Buchanan, "The Fleshly School of Poetry," *Contemporary Review*, XVIII (October 18, 1871), 334–350.

[13] Charles F. G. Masterman, *Tennyson as a Religious Teacher* (London, 1900), pp. 227 ff.

and see no more
The Stone, the Wheel, the dimly-glimmering lawns
Of that Elysium, all the hateful fires
Of torment, and the shadowy warrior glide
Along the silent field of Asphodel.
["Demeter and Persephone," lines 147–151]

With the "art for art's sake" school of Swinburne, Pater, Symonds, Wilde, and Douglas, Tennyson had great temperamental affinity, but intellectually he agreed with Trench that the artist cannot live by art alone. In preference to these middle and later Victorian writers, he fits better with Newman, Browning, Clough, and Arnold, not simply because their dates were closer to his own but because he shared their deep concern for moral and theological questions. More than any of them he was the self-conscious artist; but like them, he felt that art must rise out of and illuminate the conflict between feudal and modern England, traditional Christian doctrine and new critical approaches to doctrine and scriptures, idealism and materialism, humanism and science, and the continual perplexity of the creative individual who is in touch but out of step with his own age.

In the last years of his century and the first of ours, his work was thrust aside by that gesture with which a son asserts his own manhood by putting out of mind the personality of his father. Thomas Hardy, in the period of new realism, reflected the decline in critical favor of Tennyson's poetry immediately following his death, by a stanza in the rather grim series of toasts of "An Ancient to Ancients," 1922.

The bower we shrined to Tennyson,
        Gentlemen,
Is roof-wracked; damps there drip upon
Sagged seats, the creeper-nails are rust,
The spider is sole denizen;
Even she who voiced those rhymes is dust,
        Gentlemen!

And yet, in his way, Tennyson was a realist of scientific observation and the precise, sharp detail; and like Hardy he too felt the undying continuity of the past and was cruelly aware of that drift in the nature of the universe that tends to make men's affairs go awry. But whereas Hardy, through the lips of Elizabeth-Jane, might be content with "making limited opportunities endurable," [14] Tennyson could not endure either life or death without the hope of "Something kindlier, higher, holier," even if that Something was long coming, "for is not Earth as yet so young?" [15] Although the best he could do was "faintly trust," yet he had to find somewhere, if not in the geological-biological earth, nor in dogmatic but unproven religion, at least in his own mind and heart, a "larger hope."

Arthur J. Carr quoted Walt Whitman's discernment that Tennyson's doubts, swervings, doublings upon himself were typical of the age and went on to state that Tennyson paid a great price for being a representative Victorian poet. [16] Because he tended to keep to the midstream of his culture, a criticism of Tennyson becomes *per se* a criticism of Victorianism, and vice versa. In the twentieth century Tennyson has been largely either discarded, fragmented, or converted (Buckley's "conversion pattern").

The discarded Tennyson is described by Samuel C. Burchell, who gauged what seemed to him the general critical reaction between World War I and 1933:

Perhaps of all the great Victorians Tennyson is the one who seems at first glance most alien to the literary, moral, and social world we know today. Every age looks for an idealized image of itself in the literature of the past. In the eighteenth century writers were vain enough, or shrewd enough, to identify themselves with the Romans under Augustus; modern poets,

[14] Thomas Hardy, *The Works of Thomas Hardy*, X: *The Mayor of Casterbridge* (London, 1920), 202.

[15] *Locksley Hall Sixty Years After*, lines 160, 166.

[16] Arthur J. Carr, "Tennyson as a Modern Poet," *University of Toronto Quarterly*, XIX (July 1950), 361–382.

introspective and fascinated by the complexities of the intellectual, reveal their enthusiasm for Donne and the Metaphysicals. But even with certain obvious preferences modern critics have been willing to admit that much admirable poetry, poetry that can have a significance for the modern reader, has been written in almost every period of English history—except during the later years of the nineteenth century. At that time it would seem that talent, culture, and imagination had vanished from the world as completely as if they had never existed. For decades we have been satisfied and misled by Beerbohm's superb symbol of Victorian literature: the Laureate reading *In Memoriam* to his sovereign. [17]

Only the word "misled" gives the reader a hint that Burchell does not completely share this general opinion. Although Walker Gibson meant to praise but not to bury Tennyson, he too recognized the prevailing critical atmosphere in 1958. "The fashion today of deploring the philosophical Tennyson in favor of the melancholic or the technically graceful Tennyson should not obscure for us the experience of reading lines that carry the most detailed response in nineteenth-century poetry to the great challenge of science." [18]

Roy Basler, in 1944, stated the general criticism briefly: "Although critics have generally agreed that Tennyson is a supreme master of lyrical finesse, many have expressed grave doubts concerning his intellectual capacity and penetration." [19] When Jack Lindsay wrote his 1956 study of George Meredith, he included three references to Tennyson: "Tennysonianly false"—"Tennyson kept genteelly on the borderline of the Victorian social-economic conflicts, preening his sensibility out of the imagery-gains and techniques of the bolder spirits, till

[17] Samuel C. Burchell, "Tennyson's Dark Night," *South Atlantic Quarterly*, LIV (1933), 75.

[18] Walker Gibson, "Behind the Veil: A Distinction between Poetic and Scientific Language in Tennyson, Lyell, and Darwin," *Victorian Studies*, II (September 1958), 60–61.

[19] Roy P. Basler, "Tennyson the Psychologist," *South Atlantic Quarterly*, XLIII (April 1944), 143.

the time came when he could put his booty at the disposal of the full-fledged middle-class philistinism"—"weakly Tennysonian with false sentiment and idealist vagueness." [20] A critic has permitted a poet and his work to dissolve into epithet when the only three descriptive words he can find for a major literary figure are "false," "genteelly," and "weakly." But these critical comments represent the equation of Tennysonian and Victorian in which both terms are used only in the pejorative and invidious sense, and thus, by stereotype, discarded.

The Introduction discussed at length the fragmentation of Tennyson: Sir Harold Nicolson with five periods of Tennyson poetry, only two of which express the real Tennyson, and his theory that the poet's natural lyric genius had been tamed by a socially imposed didacticism; F. L. Lucas in mourning for Tennyson's "smothered" lyricism; W. H. Auden's neat petard about finest ear but stupidest poet. All of this stems from Nicolson's basic contention that Tennyson could be restored to public favor if he were read in excised collections. And so began the game of throwing out this *genre* and period, retaining that as relevant to the modern critical taste; deploring this, praising that; claiming this as the genuine vintage Tennyson flavor and that as written by another and lesser man who had been crushed into conformity by the public demands of his age; until Tennyson was fragmented even as the yoke of dumb oxen which Saul hewed in pieces and sent as bloody fragments "by the hands of messengers through all the coasts of Israel."

But if, like the oxen of the Old Testament Saul, he has been fragmented by some critics, he has been confused more recently with the New Testament Saul of the Damascus Road. Jerome Hamilton Buckley, in *The Victorian Temper*, placed his chapter on Tennyson (Chapter IV) between chapters on "The Spasmodic School" and "The Pattern of Conversion." Tennyson was not only the bridge between but also the exemplar of both, for *Maud* was chosen as exhibiting spasmodic impulses and *In Memoriam*, the conquest of doubt and a determined

[20] Jack Lindsay, *George Meredith* (London, 1956), pp. 35, 45, 51.

social self-dedication. This is the key to Buckley's major work *Tennyson: The Growth of a Poet*, but it does not fit as a key to the poet's total work. At least Dr. Buckley does not seek to fit Tennyson to his own age or to ours by throwing out a major part of his work. But by attempting to delineate the growth of a poet he finds himself forced to indicate major changes in one who was astonishingly the same early and late; who wrote modern and classical poetry on the same themes; who said the same things briefly in villanelles and more voluminously than in all of *Hamlet*. The recognition of precisely the same tensions in the juvenile poems and the poems written by an octogenarian parallels Arthur Carr's observation:

Tennyson's later poetry does not break from the pattern of his past. This is why he could revise his early work, as he did for the *Poems of 1842*, with as much grace and tact as if he were still in the midst of writing it for the first time; he had not moved beyond it. With thorough integrity he could publish in his later books some poems written long before and could introduce passages of this early work into poems written a half-century later. The persistence of his motives brings his later poetry back to the inescapable theses: in "The Ancient Sage" he returns to the debate of "The Two Voices," in "Lucretius" to the fierce and open warfare between erotic and conscientious impulses, in "Demeter and Persephone" to the ritual of the death and re-awakening of nature, in "Crossing the Bar" to the dream-voyages of "Morte d'Arthur" and *In Memoriam*, and in his last book to "The Death of Oenone." [21]

Buckley could, of course, have shown some development in prosody and choice of topic across the long life of the poet, but these changes would have been scarcely enough to supply evidence for a study of the growth of a poet. By claiming a major change of outlook and personality, a "conversion experience" as customarily understood, he has girded up his structure but betrayed his material. That there was no conversion experience is clearly shown by the persistence of the same motifs, doubts, ambiguities, and tensions, as much after 1850 as before.

[21] Carr, "Tennyson as a Modern Poet," pp. 361–382.

Obviously this study does not agree with the critical expedients of a discarded Tennyson, a fragmented Tennyson or a converted Tennyson. Instead it finds a critical clue in the central axiom of the Gestalt psychology, which had its beginnings with Christian von Ehrenfels in 1890, and its applications to the higher mental processes during the first four decades of our own century: "The whole is greater than the sum of its parts." This suggests that there is a greater Tennyson who is obscured and ignored in the rush to stake out one era or one type of poem as "the real Tennyson," "the best of Tennyson," "the part of Tennyson which speaks to the twentieth century." If this is so, then the real Tennyson includes everything he ever wrote, both as individual pieces and in their larger significance as determinative parts of a meaningful whole. Joyce Green sounds very sensible when she says, "It is impossible to do Tennyson justice without realizing that he was a poet of wide and varied capacity, who saw no anomaly in offering his readers the perfected fruit of many different moods." [22]

If we follow this policy of simple acceptance of all the poet's work, what shall be done with the diverse strands which often seem to pull in different directions? The treatment recommended in this paper is not the choice of one strand—all others being treated as impostors—but the selection of pairs within types that fit together, not in agreement but in the polarity of disagreement. Other than in its nonrational cults, the modern philosophic thought world is erected upon a neat Hegelianism: Thesis-Antithesis-Synthesis. But although for every thesis there must be an antithesis, for many of the resulting tensions there are no syntheses at all. In the tensions between the real and the ideal, faith and doubt, male and female, domesticity and sexual freedom—there can be no syntheses. To release such tensions is to destroy life. This is what happens to Dr. Buckley's otherwise admirable chapters IV, "The Victorian Temper" and VI, "Tennyson." He is sensitive to the tension between what

[22] Joyce Green, "Tennyson's Development During the 'Ten Years' Silence' (1832–1842)," *PMLA* (1951), p. 684.

he somewhat exaggeratedly calls the "spasmodic" impulse and the contrary mood of antiromanticism. But instead of leaving the living tension there, he resolves it by making the second the successor to the first; and the dynamic slackens, the meaning sags. A doubly "postwar generation" has discovered that the *condition humaine* is the struggle with antinomies that cannot be reconciled. We become adepts at living with opposites, and our native climate is compromise. Doubtless any simple definition of "existentialism" would include a statement of the intractable and unresolvable nature of the basic human problems. The word denotes a philosophy which places against the claims of the ideal the actual, and which tests all ideological arrogations by the ordinary conditions of day-by-day existence. Thus its doctrine of man is akin to neo-orthodoxy and its dedication to deeds is a modern stoicism. Man is subsumed by the lowest common denominator, and circumstances are dealt with bravely without the slightest illusion of ultimate solution or success.

Tennyson's poems exhibit recessive tendencies as negative lodestones that have positive counterparts which draw the poet back into the world. In the working out of these two opposing attractions is found the development of one whom Joyce Green calls "a poet pre-eminently equipped to spiritualize the apparently commonplace." [23] The opposition also works in the other direction of pouring passionate longing into the ideal world of the poetic imagination and the visionary experience of another world. But this opposition is neither a betrayal of the poet's true task nor a permanent identification of his real interest. Instead both the tendency to retreat and the conscience-compulsion to return are parts of a natural and continuing characteristic which greatly enriched the poet's personality and verse. For T. H. Huxley the conscience might be merely a social monitor, the voice of social obligation, but for Tennyson the conscience arose from the primitive and powerful depths of the unconscious and emerged into artistic

[23] *Ibid.*

creation as a mixture of irreconcilable motives and contesting values. Because he met society and the world with a divided will, Tennyson kept finding himself thrust off for relief into either despair of any social hope, or fantasy which escapes the pressures of a recalcitrant world.

Swinburne's parody of "The Higher Pantheism" points up, on a lighter level, Tennyson's problem with multileveled reality. "The Higher Pantheism in a Nutshell," 1880, is at first sight disappointing because there is so little resemblance to its subject in form, meter or style. But Swinburne does capture the unresolved tension between the real and the ideal. If the two verses are placed side by side, the quality of almost pathological unresolvedness becomes plain:

> Is not the Vision He, though He be not that which He
> seems?
> Dreams are true while they last, and do we not live in
> dreams?   (Tennyson)

> One, who is not, we see; but one, whom we see not, is.
> Surely this is not that; but that is assuredly this.
>   (Swinburne)

The key to the brilliance of the Swinburnian parody is the the capture of appearance which is not real and reality which cannot appear. It offers the comfort and assurance of words like "surely" and "assuredly," but defies any reader to discover of just what he is to be assured. Tennyson came very close to a parody of his own dubiety in Arthur's address to the kitchen-knave in "Gareth and Lynette":

> "Friend, whether thou be kitchen-knave, or not
> Or whether it be the maiden's fantasy,
> Or whether she be mad, or else the King,
> Or both or neither, or thyself be mad,
> I ask not. . . ." [lines 852–856]

The man to whom the matter of identity was so important that he could slip into a trance by the simple expedient of murmuring his name over and over again, was the son of a father who was so unsure of his identity that, about to call on a parishioner, he suddenly forgot his own name. Excusing himself, he hastened home to ask his wife. On the way he was hailed by a neighbor who addressed him by name. The good rector was perfectly satisfied and retraced his steps to complete his call with a freshly verified identity.

Tennyson was constantly working with the shifting planes of physical appearance, spiritual reality, personal identity and poetic imagination—all in the focus of the problem they present to faith and life. He desired to assure himself and others, but because he could never release either pole of his own tensions, he could never reach the static condition of perfect assurance or denial. A key pattern emerges from his poetry: of the opposites we have been noting, the truth may be neither one, or more likely it may be both; the one thing it cannot be is *either one*. In poetic form, this tends to create a twin-leveled reality with wistful longings and emotional strivings for a resolution which cannot come about in the face of the two balanced lists of contradictory data.

One of the dominant characteristics of Tennyson which the critics seem to miss is his extraordinarily explicit honesty, so that at the moment we expect affirmation he affirms, but at the same time he confesses that he is not so sure as the words might sound. Thus the Tennyson poem tends to become a kind of dialogue, a juxtaposition of unlikes which, like modern surrealism, reveals the character of each and both, not statically but as the very tension between powerful and unresolvable opposites. And the agony with which he cries from the toils of opposing tendencies proclaims his magnificent honesty and his kinship with the torn and divided men of all ages.

The last time Guinevere saw Arthur, as he moved away into the mists, Tennyson characteristically depicted an ambiguous figure.

> she did not see the face,
> Which then was as an angel's, but she saw,
> Wet with the mists and smitten by the lights,
> The Dragon of the great Pendragonship
> Blaze, making all the night a steam of fire.

And even then he turn'd; and more and more
The moony vapor rolling round the King,
Who seem'd the phantom of a giant in it,
Enwound him fold by fold, and made him gray
And grayer, till himself became as mist
Before her, moving ghostlike to his doom.

["Guinevere," lines 591–601]

If this is what she saw, who had reason to know him well, then who, in the final analysis, was Arthur—angel or man, the mist or the light, supernatural ruler or natural king, the damp night or the warm fire, giant or phantom, real or unreal? To answer the question by making him any half of these pairs of contrasting and therefore complementary qualities is to destroy the fullest imagery and meaning of the *Idylls of the King*. In exactly the same sense, to assert that Tennyson is essentially lyric rather than didactic, sensuous rather than idealistic, a skeptic rather than a Christian believer, a secluded artist rather than life's concerned participant is to destroy the basis in tension for the fullest interpretation of the whole body of his work.

When E. M. Forster published his novel *Howards End*, he used the enigmatic little phrase, "Only connect," as a subtitle or motto. Within the text he gave two illustrations of the kind of connection of which he was speaking. First, he says that truth is not "half-way between" the two realms of matter and spirit, but "continuous excursions into either realm." Second, he assures those who deal with the two realms that they need "only connect, and the beast and the monk, robbed of the isolation that is life to either, will die." Tennyson could have pointed out that these two statements are somewhat contradictory. He too wanted the ape and tiger to die, but he had learned from the rhythm of his own life of retreat and return that "continuous excursions" provide the real and only possible connection. Neither monk nor beast will die, both will live and exert mutually exclusive pressures and life will somehow have to maintain not peace but an armed truce between.

But beyond their probable disagreements, it is fascinating to note that this twentieth-century countryman of the nineteenth-century poet is thinking along the very same lines, in almost the same terms, and with closely similar conclusions. In 1950, Arthur Carr called Tennyson "our true precursor. He shows and hides, as if in embryo, a master theme of Joyce's *Ulysses*— the accentuated and moody self-consciousness and the sense of loss that mark Stephen Dedalus. He forecasts Yeats' interest in the private myth. He apprehended in advance of Aldous Huxley the uses of mysticism to castigate materialistic culture. And in *Maud*, at least, he prepared the way for the verse of Eliot's 'Preludes' and 'Prufrock.' At some crucial points Tennyson is a modern poet, and there are compelling reasons why we should try to comprehend him. Our uneasiness, our reluctance to acknowledge the relationship is understandable, and it explains how little we advance towards seeing what Tennyson's poetry is like." [24]

Douglas Bush noted the lack of structure in some of Tennyson's classical poems, but he found a succession of splendid moments.[25] H. M. McLuhan acknowledges the truth of the observation but claims that "it is precisely his fidelity to the vivisection of isolated moments that links Tennyson to the greatest work of his time and of ours. . . . It is to be related to the tendency to abandon succession for simultaneity when our instruments of observation acquired speed and precision. . . . Lineal succession as a concept of order cannot hold the same absolute position in our nuclear consciousness as it did in the great age of mechanism that stretches from Gutenberg to Darwin." [26]

When Tennyson wrote "Crossing the Bar" in his eighty-first year, his son Hallam exclaimed, "That is the crown of

[24] Carr, "Tennyson as a Modern Poet," pp. 361–382.

[25] Douglas Bush, *Mythology and the Romantic Tradition* (Cambridge, Mass., 1937), pp. 199 ff.

[26] H. M. McLuhan, "Tennyson and the Romantic Epic," in John Killham (ed.), *Critical Essays on the Poetry of Tennyson* (London, 1960), p. 93.

your life's work." Then only a few days before his death, Tennyson enjoined Hallam solemnly, "Mind you put 'Crossing the Bar' at the end of all editions of my poems.'" [27] No doubt the poet felt that this finial place would be appropriate for such a poem because of its valedictory nature and its appeal to Christian sentiment. But there is another sense in which it is most appropriate, in that it picks up, in what was undoubtedly an unconscious medley, many of the themes we have been tracing through the poetic labors of seventy years. It was written at a time when he begged his old friend Jowett, if he came to visit him, not to "consult with him or argue with him, as was his wont, on points of philosophy or religious doubt." He preferred to smoke his pipe, sink down into the reflections of the years and perhaps talk, if at all, with quiet old peasants "from whom he always tried to ascertain their thoughts upon death and the future life." [28] Like Wordsworth, he was not above probing the naïve and spontaneous faith of the very young. He asked Sophia Palmer, the adolescent daughter of his Anglo-Catholic friend Lord Selborne, what she would think if she saw the bodies of her parents rotting in the grave. She replied that she would feel they were still alive. "'You are sure?' he pressed her; and on her repeating her assurance, 'Ah well!' he said, with rather pathetic relief, 'Yes, I do hold it so. I have tried to say it—to show it—that the body is the husk— the shell. But at times these new lights, this science wearies and perplexes me; yet I know they cannot reach, cannot explain. . . .'" [29]

The setting of "Crossing the Bar" is sunset and the evening star invoked in "The Poet's Song" and "The Hesperides" as the creative hour for the poet, and in *In Memoriam* (CXXI) as the symbol of death which is also implicit resurrection— Hesper-Phospher. If at this evening hour the poet received "one clear call" it was the only single, clear, unified voice he

[27] Tennyson (Hallam), II, 367.
[28] *Ibid.*, pp. 211, 418.
[29] Tennyson (Charles), *Tennyson*, p. 460.

had ever heard. It is clear in that it is the signal for action, in this case departure; but it is not clear as to destination. The departure is upon and the destination is far beyond the element Tennyson most loved and most made his own, the sea—"may there by no moaning of the bar, / When I put out to sea." The imagery is reminiscent of those other water-voyages to death and perhaps something beyond, "The Lady of Shalott," "The Voyage," "Ulysses," *In Memoriam*, and "The Passing of Arthur." His irrepressible instinct for contrast swells up in a tide which moves but seems asleep, in a mounting of great waves which make no sound and neither froth nor foam. With his fondness for the vague and indefinite, he describes the turning home of that which came from the "boundless deep." Where is "home"; what is "that"; is the "boundless deep" the sea or the infinite space beyond? Twilight comes with the ringing of the evening bell and in its clanging we hear the echoes of the bells at Somersby and at High Beech and the tocsin beat of those "wild bells" that rang "to the wild skies." But after the bell, the dark—the dark in which time no longer flows in the night, and the sleeper is fretted by the sharp-headed worm. But let the embarcation be without sadness; let Ulysses embark at evening to sail beyond the sunset—the waves break and the heart breaks only for the death of a friend.[30] ". . . from out our bourne of Time and Place"—what a Time and what a Place have been his! Shrinking from the battle, yet he courageously fought the specters of materialism and naturalism, cynicism and death, doubt and despair. His word was not "trampled by the populace underfoot"[31] and he spoke the truth that many men believed. Time and tide are at the flood and the aged prophet wishes he were "gather'd to" his "rest," where his eyes might find the men he knew, loved, and lost. But when he does embark and his little life floats out to the great sea, when the last bar of sand and the last reminder of earth are past, will he find himself in the Hands of God? With characteristic and

[30] "Break, Break, Break."
[31] "Tiresias."

life-long dubiety he says, "I hope to see my Pilot face to face."
This is not affirmation, it is still trusting the "larger hope,"
looking with blind eyes at "one far height in one far-shining
fire," longing amidst social chaos for the "one far-off divine
event" which will reduce to cosmos. In the language of wist-
fulness, he hopes to see—whom? He explained to Hallam
that by Pilot he meant "That Divine and Unseen Who is
always guiding us." [32] Read one way, this clause supplies a
thoroughly satisfying answer and rings with the genuine tone
of orthodox belief in a guiding Providence. But scrutinized
more carefully the statement is notable in that it avoids the use
of the name of God, or of His Son, and the poem never
specifically mentions the doctrine of immortality.

Bedivere watched Arthur sail away in the barge with the
dark damsels and saw

> Or thought he saw, the speck that bare the King,
> Down that long water opening on the deep
> Somewhere far off, pass on and on, and go
> From less to less and vanish into light.
>   ["The Passing of Arthur," lines 465–468]

Guinevere watched as the "moony vapor"

> Enwound him fold by fold, and made him gray
> And grayer, till himself became as mist
> Before her, moving ghostlike to his doom.
>   ["Guinevere," lines 599–601]

We watch Tennyson borne away by the flood, carried upon a
force he neither directs nor opposes, faintly sustained by a
yearning hope.

> Sunset and evening star,
>   And one clear call for me!
> And may there be no moaning of the bar,
>   When I put out to sea.

[32] Tennyson (Hallam), *Memoir*, II, 367.

But such a tide as moving seems asleep,
    Too full for sound and foam,
When that which drew from out the boundless deep
    Turns again home.

Twilight and evening bell,
    And after that the dark!
And may there be no sadness of farewell,
    When I embark;

For tho' from out our bourne of Time and Place
    The flood may bear me far,
I hope to see my Pilot face to face
    When I have crost the bar.

Bibliography

BOOKS

ALIGHIERI, DANTE. *The Divine Comedy*. Translated by Henry F. Cary. Garden City: Doubleday, 1947.

AUDEN, WYSTAN HUGH. Introduction, Charles Pierre Baudelaire, *Intimate Journals*. Hollywood: Marcel Rodd, 1947.

————. Introduction, *A Selection from the Poems of Alfred, Lord Tennyson*. Garden City: Doubleday, 1944.

AUGUSTINE, SAINT. *Confessions*. Translated by E. B. Pusey. London J. M. Dent & Sons, 1946.

BAGEHOT, WALTER. "Wordsworth, Tennyson and Browning" (1864), in *English Critical Essays: Nineteenth Century*. Edited by Edmund D. Jones. Oxford: Oxford University Press, 1945.

BAUGH, ALBERT C. *A Literary History of England*. Vol. IV., Samuel C. Chew. *The Nineteenth Century and After, 1789–1939*. New York: Appleton-Century-Crofts, 1948.

BAUM, PAULL F. *Tennyson Sixty Years After*. Chapel Hill: University of North Carolina Press, 1948.

BOZMAN, MILDRED. Introduction, *Poems of Alfred Tennyson*. New York: E. P. Dutton, 1949.

BREDVOLD, LOUIS IGNATIUS. *The Intellectual Milieu of John Dryden*. Ann Arbor: University of Michigan Press, 1934.

BRIGHTWELL, E. BARRON. *A Concordance to the Entire Works of Alfred Tennyson*. London: George Routledge & Sons, 1869.

BRISSENDEN, R. F. *Samuel Richardson*. London: British Books, David McKay, 1958.

BROOKE, STOPFORD A. *Tennyson: His Art and Relation to Modern Life*. London and New York: G. P. Putnam's Sons, 1899.

BROOKFIELD, FRANCES M. *The Cambridge "Apostles."* New York: Charles Scribner's Sons, 1907.

BROOKS, CLEANTH. *Modern Poetry and the Tradition.* Chapel Hill: University of North Carolina Press, 1939.

———. *The Well Wrought Urn: Studies in the Structure of Poetry.* New York: Harcourt, Brace, 1947.

BUCKLER, WILLIAM E. Introduction, Thomas Hardy, *Jude the Obscure.* New York: Dell Publishing Co., 1959.

BUCKLEY, JEROME HAMILTON. *The Victorian Temper: A Study in Literary Culture.* Cambridge, Massachusetts: Harvard University Press, 1951.

———. *Tennyson: The Growth of a Poet.* Cambridge, Massachusetts: Harvard University Press, 1960.

BUSH, DOUGLAS. *Mythology and the Romantic Tradition.* Cambridge, Massachusetts: Harvard University Press, 1937.

CECIL, LORD DAVID. *Melbourne.* New York: Grosset & Dunlap, 1954.

COLERIDGE, SAMUEL TAYLOR. *Biographia Literaria.* London: J. M. Dent & Sons, 1949.

CRUSE, AMY. *The Victorians and Their Reading.* Boston: Houghton Mifflin, 1935.

CUNLIFFE, JOHN WILLIAM. *Pictured History of English Literature.* New York and London: Appleton-Century-Crofts, 1933.

DAVIDSON, THOMAS. *Prolegomena to "In Memoriam."* Boston: Houghton Mifflin, 1897.

DARWIN, CHARLES. *The Voyage of the Beagle.* New York: P. F. Collier & Son, 1909. *The Harvard Classics,* XXIX, Edited by Charles W. Eliot.

DONNE, JOHN. *The Divine Poems.* Edited by Helen Gardner. Oxford: Oxford University Press, 1952.

ELIOT, THOMAS STEARNS. *Complete Poems and Plays.* New York: Harcourt, Brace, 1952.

———. *Essays, Ancient and Modern.* New York: Harcourt, Brace, 1936.

ELTON, OLIVER. *A Survey of English Literature.* Vols. III, IV. London: Macmillan, 1924.

FAIRCHILD, HOXIE NEALE. *Religious Trends in English Poetry: 1830–1880.* New York: Columbia University Press, 1957.

FAUSSET, HUGH I'ANSON. *Tennyson: A Modern Portrait*. London: Selwyn & Blount, 1923. Also in Travellers' Library, London: Jonathan Cape, 1929.

FITZGERALD, EDWARD. *Letters and Literary Remains*. London and New York: Doubleday, 1902–1903.

FROUDE, JAMES ANTHONY. *Thomas Carlyle: A History of His Life in London*. New York: Harper & Bros., 1910.

GASKELL, ELISABETH CLEGHORNE. *Cranford*. New York: Macmillan, 1891.

GATTY, ALFRED. *A Key to Lord Tennyson's "In Memoriam."* London: G. Bell & Sons, 1885.

GENUNG, JOHN F. *Tennyson's "In Memoriam": Its Purpose and Its Structure*. Boston: Houghton Mifflin, 1894.

GROSART, ALEXANDER B. (ed.). *The Prose Works of William Wordsworth*. London, 1876.

HARDY, THOMAS. *The Works of Thomas Hardy*. Vol. X: *The Mayor of Casterbridge*. London: Macmillan, 1920.

ISHERWOOD, CHRISTOPHER. Introduction, Charles Pierre Baudelaire, *Intimate Journals*. Hollywood: Marcel Rodd, 1947.

JACOBS, JOSEPH. *Tennyson and "In Memoriam."* London: David Nutt, 1892.

JOHNSON, EDWARD DUDLEY HUME. *The Alien Vision of Victorian Poetry*. Princeton: Princeton University Press, 1952.

JONES, RICHARD. *The Growth of the "Idylls of the King."* Philadelphia: J. B. Lippincott, 1895.

KER, WILLIAM PATON. *Tennyson*. The Leslie Stephen Lecture. Cambridge: Cambridge University Press, 1909.

KILLHAM, JOHN. *Tennyson and "The Princess": Reflections of an Age*. London: Athlone Press, 1958.

――――. (ed.). *Critical Essays on the Poetry of Tennyson*. New York: Barnes & Noble, 1960. See also names of individual contributors in "Articles."

KRONENBERGER, LOUIS (ed.). *The Portable Johnson & Boswell*. New York: Macmillan, 1955.

LANGBAUM, ROBERT. *The Poetry of Experience*. London: Chatto & Windus, 1957.

LEGOUIS, EMILE, and LOUIS CAZAMIAN. *A History of English Literature*. Vol. II. New York: Macmillan, 1927.

LINDSAY, JACK. *George Meredith.* London: John Lane, The Bodley Head, 1956.

LUCAS, FRANK LAURENCE. *Ten Victorian Poets.* New York: Macmillan, 1948.

———. *Tennyson.* London, New York, Toronto: Longmans, Green, 1957.

LYELL, CHARLES. *Travels in North America.* London: John Murray, 1845.

MALORY, SIR THOMAS. *Morte d'Arthur.* Edited by Thomas Wright. London: Reeves and Turner, 1889.

MARTINEAU, JAMES. *Essays, Philosophical and Theological.* New York: Longmans, Green, 1875.

MASTERMAN, CHARLES F. G. *Tennyson as a Religious Teacher.* London: Methuen, 1900.

MOTTER, T. H. VAIL (ed.). *The Writings of Arthur Hallam.* New York: Modern Language Association of America, 1943.

NICOLSON, SIR HAROLD. *Tennyson: Aspects of His Life, Character and Poetry.* Boston and New York: Houghton Mifflin, 1922.

NICOLSON, MARJORIE H. (ed.). *Selected Poems of Alfred Tennyson.* Boston: Houghton Mifflin, 1924.

NORTON, C. E. (ed.). *The Correspondence of Thomas Carlyle and Ralph Waldo Emerson.* Boston: Ticknor, 1894.

NOYES, RUSSELL (ed.). *English Romantic Poetry and Prose.* New York: Oxford University Press, 1956.

PADEN, WILLIAM DOREMUS. *Tennyson in Egypt: A Study of the Imagery in His Earlier Work.* Lawrence: University of Kansas Press, 1922.

PATER, WALTER. "Style." *Appreciations.* London: Macmillan, 1889.

SAINTSBURY, GEORGE. *A History of Nineteenth-Century Literature.* New York and London: Macmillan, 1896.

SHAKESPEARE, WILLIAM. *The Complete Works.* Edited by G. B. Harrison. New York: Harcourt, Brace, 1952.

SHANNON, EDGAR FINLEY, JR. *Tennyson and the Reviewers.* Cambridge, Massachusetts: Harvard University Press, 1952.

SHELLEY, PERCY BYSSHE. *Literary and Philosophical Criticism.* London: Henry Frowde, 1909.

SHELLEY, PERCY BYSSHE. *The Complete Poetical Works of Percy Bysshe Shelley*. Edited by Thomas Hutchinson. London: Geoffrey Cumberlege, Oxford University Press, 1948.

STANFORD, WILLIAM BEDELL. *The Ulysses Theme: A Study in the Adaptability of a Traditional Hero*. Oxford: B. H. Blackwell, 1954.

STEDMAN, EDMUND CLARENCE. *Victorian Poets*. Boston: Houghton Mifflin, 1903.

SWIFT, JONATHAN. *The Portable Swift*. Edited by Carl Van Doren, *Travels Into Several Remote Nations of the World, by Lemuel Gulliver*. New York: Viking Press, 1948.

SWINBURNE, ALGERNON CHARLES. *Miscellanies*. London: Chatto & Windus, 1895.

TENNYSON, ALFRED. *The Devil and the Lady*. London: Macmillan, 1930.

————. *Idylls of the King*. Philadelphia: J. B. Lippincott, 1920.

————. *The Poetic and Dramatic Works of Alfred, Lord Tennyson*. Edited by William James Rolfe. Boston and New York: Houghton Mifflin, 1898.

TENNYSON, CHARLES B. L. *Alfred Tennyson*. New York: Macmillan, 1949.

TENNYSON, HALLAM. *Alfred, Lord Tennyson: A Memoir by His Son*. New York: Macmillan, 1897.

———— (ed.). *Works of Alfred, Lord Tennyson*. Annotated by the author. New York: Macmillan, 1908.

TENNYSON, HALLAM, LORD (ed.). *Tennyson and His Friends*. London: Macmillan, 1911.

TERHUNE, A. McKINLEY. *Life of Edward FitzGerald*. New Haven: Yale University Press, 1947.

THACKERAY, WILLIAM MAKEPEACE. *The Works of William Makepeace Thackeray*. Vol. VI: *The Newcomes*. London: Smith, Elder, 1907.

TINDALL, WILLIAM YORK. *Forces in Modern British Literature*. New York: Alfred A. Knopf, 1947.

TRENCH, M. *Richard Chenevix Trench, Archbishop: Letters and Memorials*. London, 1888.

VAN DYKE, HENRY, and D. LAURENCE CHAMBERS (eds.). *Poems of Tennyson*. Boston: Ginn, 1903.

WALKER, HUGH. *The Literature of the Victorian Era.* London: Cambridge University Press, 1910.

WELBY, THOMAS EARLE. *A Study of Swinburne.* New York: George H. Doran, 1926.

WHITE, HELEN C., RUTH C. WALLERSTEIN, and RICHARD QUINTANA (eds.). *Seventeenth-Century Verse and Prose.* New York: Macmillan, 1957.

WILSON, DAVID ALEC. *Carlyle.* New York: E. P. Dutton, 1923–1934.

WOLFE, THOMAS. *Look Homeward, Angel.* New York: Charles Scribner's Sons, 1929.

WOODS, GEORGE BENJAMIN, and JEROME HAMILTON BUCKLEY (eds.). *Poetry of the Victorian Period.* New York: Scott, Foresman, 1955.

ARTICLES

Basler, Roy P., "Tennyson the Psychologist," *South Atlantic Quarterly*, XLIII (April 1944), 143–159.

Buchanan, R. W., "The Fleshly School of Poetry," *Contemporary Review*, XVIII (October 18, 1871), 334–350.

Burchell, Samuel C., "Tennyson's 'Allegory in the Distance,'" *Publications of the Modern Language Association*, LXVIII (1953), 418–424.

――――, "Tennyson's Dark Night," *South Atlantic Quarterly*, LIV (January 1955), 75–81.

Carr, Arthur J., "Tennyson as a Modern Poet," *University of Toronto Quarterly*, XIX (July 1950), 361–382.

Chiasson, E. J., "Tennyson's 'Ulysses'—a Re-Interpretation," in John Killham (ed.): *Critical Essays on the Poetry of Tennyson* (London, 1960).

de Vere, Aubrey, "Review on Shelley [*The Poetical Works*], Milnes [*Life of Keats*], and Tennyson [*Poems, 1842*]," *Edinburgh Review*, XC (July–October 1849), 388.

"The Eglinton Tournament," *Record*, III, 36; *Examiner*, XXX (July 14, 1839), 441; (September 1, 1839), 555; (September 8, 1839), 552.

Felton, C. C., *The Christian Examiner*, XXXIII (1842), 237.

Fox, Canon Adam, "Tennyson's Elegy," *Spectator*, CLXXXIV (June 16, 1950), 816–817.

Gibson, Walker, "Behind the Veil: A Distinction Between Poetic and Scientific Language in Tennyson, Lyell, and Darwin," *Victorian Studies*, II (September 1958), 60–68.

Gladstone, William Ewart, *Nineteenth Century* XXI (January 1887), I.

———, "Review of *In Memoriam*," *Gleanings of Past Years*. New York, 1886.

Green, Joyce, "Tennyson's Development During the 'Ten Years' Silence' (1832–1842)," *Publications of the Modern Language Association*, LXVI (1951), 662–697.

Groom, Bernard, "On the Diction of Tennyson, Browning and Arnold," *Society for Pure English*, Tract No. LIII (Oxford, 1939), 93–105.

Gwynn, Stephen, "The Return to Tennyson," *Spectator*, CLXXVI (March 22, 1946), 292–293.

Hogg's Weekly Instructor, Editorial, VI (December 25, 1847), 273.

Howell, A. C., "Tennyson's 'Palace of Art'—an Interpretation," *Studies in Philology*, XXXIII (July 1936), 507–522.

Huxley, Thomas Henry, "Tennyson" (poem), *Nineteenth Century*, XXXII (November 1892), 831.

Johnson, W. Stacy, "The Theme of Marriage in Tennyson," *Victorian Newsletter*, XII (Fall 1957), 8–14.

Korg, Jacob, "The Pattern of Fatality in Tennyson's Poetry," *Victorian Newsletter*, XIV (Fall 1958), 8–11.

Krause, Anna, "Unamuno and Tennyson," *Comparative Literature*, VIII (Spring 1956), 122–135.

MacEachen, Dugald B., "Tennyson and the Sonnet," *Victorian Newsletter*, XIV (Fall 1958), 6.

MacLaren, Malcolm, "Tennyson's Epicurean Lotos-Eaters," *Classical Journal*, (March 1961), pp. 259–267.

McLuhan, H. M., "Tennyson and the Romantic Epic," in John Killham (ed.) : *Critical Essays on the Poetry of Tennyson* (London, 1960).

Mooney, E. A., "A Note on Astronomy in Tennyson's *The Princess*," *Modern Language Notes*, LXIV (1949), 98–102.

Nicolson, Sir Harold, "Marginal Comment," *Spectator*, CLXIX (October 9, 1942), 334.

Peter, John, "*Murder in the Cathedral*," *Sewanee Review*, LXI (July 1953), 362–383.

Preyer, Robert, "Tennyson as an Oracular Poet," *Modern Philology*, LV (May 1958), 239–251.

Priestley, F. E. D., "Tennyson's Idylls," in John Killham (ed.): *Critical Essays on the Poetry of Tennyson* (London, 1960).

Robson, W. W., "The Dilemma of Tennyson," in John Killham (ed.): *Critical Essays on the Poetry of Tennyson* (London, 1960).

Sanders, Charles Richard, "Carlyle and Tennyson," *Publications of the Modern Language Association*, LXXVI (March 1961), 82–97.

Spedding, James, "Mr. Tennyson's Poems: A Review," *Edinburgh Review*, LXXVII (1843), 203–204.

Stange, G. Robert, "Tennyson's Mythology—a Study of 'Demeter and Persephone,'" *English Literary History*, XXI (March 1954), 67–80.

———, "Tennyson's Garden of Art: A Study of 'The Hesperides,'" *Publications of the Modern Language Association*, LXVII (September 1952), 732–743.

Stevenson, Lionel, "The 'High-Born Maiden' Symbol in Tennyson," *Publications of the Modern Language Association*, LXIII (March–June 1948), 234–243.

Young, George M., "The Age of Tennyson," Warton Lecture, *Proceedings of the British Academy*, XXV (1939).

Index

[*The Data Processing Division of the University of South Florida kindly assisted in the preparation of this index.*]

211